George Eliot: A Very Short Introduction

VERY SHORT INTRODUCTIONS are for anyone wanting a stimulating and accessible way into a new subject. They are written by experts, and have been translated into more than 45 different languages.

The series began in 1995, and now covers a wide variety of topics in every discipline. The VSI library currently contains over 750 volumes—a Very Short Introduction to everything from Psychology and Philosophy of Science to American History and Relativity—and continues to grow in every subject area.

Very Short Introductions available now:

ABOLITIONISM Richard S. Newman
THE ABRAHAMIC RELIGIONS
    Charles L. Cohen
ACCOUNTING Christopher Nobes
ADDICTION Keith Humphreys
ADOLESCENCE Peter K. Smith
THEODOR W. ADORNO
    Andrew Bowie
ADVERTISING Winston Fletcher
AERIAL WARFARE Frank Ledwidge
AESTHETICS Bence Nanay
AFRICAN AMERICAN HISTORY
    Jonathan Scott Holloway
AFRICAN AMERICAN RELIGION
    Eddie S. Glaude Jr.
AFRICAN HISTORY John Parker and
    Richard Rathbone
AFRICAN POLITICS Ian Taylor
AFRICAN RELIGIONS
    Jacob K. Olupona
AGEING Nancy A. Pachana
AGNOSTICISM Robin Le Poidevin
AGRICULTURE Paul Brassley and
    Richard Soffe
ALEXANDER THE GREAT
    Hugh Bowden
ALGEBRA Peter M. Higgins
AMERICAN BUSINESS HISTORY
    Walter A. Friedman
AMERICAN CULTURAL HISTORY
    Eric Avila
AMERICAN FOREIGN RELATIONS
    Andrew Preston
AMERICAN HISTORY Paul S. Boyer

AMERICAN IMMIGRATION
    David A. Gerber
AMERICAN INTELLECTUAL
    HISTORY
    Jennifer Ratner-Rosenhagen
THE AMERICAN JUDICIAL SYSTEM
    Charles L. Zelden
AMERICAN LEGAL HISTORY
    G. Edward White
AMERICAN MILITARY HISTORY
    Joseph T. Glatthaar
AMERICAN NAVAL HISTORY
    Craig L. Symonds
AMERICAN POETRY David Caplan
AMERICAN POLITICAL HISTORY
    Donald Critchlow
AMERICAN POLITICAL PARTIES
    AND ELECTIONS L. Sandy Maisel
AMERICAN POLITICS
    Richard M. Valelly
THE AMERICAN PRESIDENCY
    Charles O. Jones
THE AMERICAN REVOLUTION
    Robert J. Allison
AMERICAN SLAVERY
    Heather Andrea Williams
THE AMERICAN SOUTH
    Charles Reagan Wilson
THE AMERICAN WEST
    Stephen Aron
AMERICAN WOMEN'S HISTORY
    Susan Ware
AMPHIBIANS T. S. Kemp
ANAESTHESIA Aidan O'Donnell

Available soon:

For more information visit our website

www.oup.com/vsi/

Juliette Atkinson

GEORGE ELIOT

A Very Short Introduction

OXFORD
UNIVERSITY PRESS

OXFORD
UNIVERSITY PRESS

Great Clarendon Street, Oxford, OX2 6DP,
United Kingdom

Oxford University Press is a department of the University of Oxford.
It furthers the University's objective of excellence in research, scholarship,
and education by publishing worldwide. Oxford is a registered trade mark of
Oxford University Press in the UK and in certain other countries

Published in the United States of America by Oxford University Press
198 Madison Avenue, New York, NY 10016, United States of America

British Library Cataloguing in Publication Data
Data available

Library of Congress Control Number: 2024948802

ISBN 9780198864325

DOI: 10.1093/9780191896408.001.0001

Printed and bound by
CPI Group (UK) Ltd, Croydon, CR0 4YY

The manufacturer's authorised representative in the EU for product safety is Oxford University
Press España S.A. of El Parque Empresarial San Fernando de Henares,
Avenida de Castilla, 2 – 28830 Madrid (www.oup.es/en or product.safety@oup.com).
OUP España S.A. also acts as importer into Spain of products made by the manufacturer.

For Tom

Contents

List of illustrations

Note on editions

Quotations from Eliot's fiction have been taken from the Oxford World's Classics editions published by Oxford University Press, as follows:

1857   *Scenes of Clerical Life*, ed. Thomas A. Noble, introduction and notes by Josie Billington (2015).

1859   *Adam Bede*, ed. Carol A. Martin (2008).

1859   'The Lifted Veil', in *The Lifted Veil and Brother Jacob*, ed. Helen Small (2009).

1860   *The Mill on the Floss*, ed. Gordon S. Haight, introduction and notes by Juliette Atkinson (2015).

1861   *Silas Marner: The Weaver of Raveloe*, ed. Juliette Atkinson (2017).

1862–3   *Romola*, ed. Andrew Brown (1998).

1864   'Brother Jacob' in *The Lifted Veil and Brother Jacob*, ed. Helen Small (2009).

1866   *Felix Holt, The Radical*, ed. Fred C. Thompson (1988).

1871–2   *Middlemarch: A Study of Provincial Life*, ed. David Carroll, with an introduction by David Russell (2019).

1876   *Daniel Deronda*, ed. Graham Handley, with an introduction by K. M. Newton (2014).

Quotations from other works by Eliot have been taken from the following editions:

1846   translation of David Friedrich Strauss, *The Life of Jesus, Critically Examined* (*Das Leben Jesu, kritisch bearbeitet,* 1835–6) (London: Chapman, Brothers, 1846), 3 vols.

1854   translation of Ludwig Feuerbach, *The Essence of Christianity* (*Das Wesen des Christentums,* 1841) (London: John Chapman, 1854).

1856   translation of Spinoza, *Ethics* (*Ethica ordine geometrico demonstrata,* 1677), first published in 1981, ed. Clare Carlisle (Princeton: Princeton University Press, 2020).

1879   *Impressions of Theophrastus Such,* ed. Nancy Henry (London: William Pickering, 1994).

Essays of George Eliot, ed. Thomas Pinney (London: Routledge and Kegan Paul, 1963). Cited as *Essays* in *References* section.

The Journals of George Eliot, ed. Margaret Harris and Judith Johnston (Cambridge: Cambridge University Press, 1998). Cited as *Journals* in *References* section.

Quotations from Eliot's letters have been taken from *The George Eliot Letters,* 9 vols, ed. Gordon S. Haight (New Haven: Yale University Press, 1954–78), and are cited in-text by volume and page number as follows: (I.42).

Prologue

'I don't see how I can leave anything out, because I hope there is nothing that will be seen to be irrelevant to my design' (V.168). When George Eliot shared this anxiety with her publisher in 1871, they were busy calculating how best to chop up *Middlemarch* into manageable chunks for readers. Eliot was still fairly early in the process of writing the novel, so this was a little premature. It would grow to over 300,000 words.

In 2006, the critic Gillian Beer published an essay called 'What's Not in *Middlemarch*'. There are other enormous 19th-century novels: Thackeray's *Vanity Fair* is only a little shorter, while Dickens's *David Copperfield* and Trollope's *The Way We Live Now* clock in at over 350,000. But Beer's title works because, unlike these, *Middlemarch* is not just long: it seems to contain everything. Its range of interests—from science to religion and everything in between—is dazzling. It applies this intellectual breadth to the ordinary events affecting ordinary people in an ordinary town. The movement between the telescopic and the microscopic is both its subject and its form.

Leaving things out was hard for a novelist who held 'a concept of organic form far more subtle and sophisticated than any but the most astute of her reviewers expect to find in fiction', as David

Carroll notes. One example: she carefully accrues images that grow naturally out of the specific setting and concerns of each novel. The water imagery that saturates *The Mill on the Floss*, for instance, is handled literally to describe a community reliant on irrigation as well as figuratively to suggest links between water and plot, fate, character, the subconscious, myth, and socio-historical change. (It also prompts her strangest clause: 'I am in love with moistness'.)

Something similar happens with weaving in *Silas Marner*, with webs in *Middlemarch*, and with games in *Daniel Deronda*. Such imagery isn't symbolic—Eliot is too wary of tidy schemas for that. Rather, it offers what she calls 'threads of connexion' and reminds us that what we hold in our hands is art and not a photograph—a recent technology with which her fiction was often compared. 'I meant everything in the book to be related to everything else there' (VI.290), she wrote of *Daniel Deronda*, exasperated by her readers' tendency to focus on the more exciting half of the plot.

Eliot's methods of composition meant that, unlike many contemporaries, she found serialization uncongenial. She was entirely unsuited to the weekly publication schedule of a novel like Dickens's *Great Expectations*, let alone the daily morsels of Dumas's *The Three Musketeers* that French readers were fed. The mad rush in which Thackeray completed his monthly instalments of *Vanity Fair*, privately hooting at readers for overlooking his mistakes ('O you donkies!'), would have appalled her. She often made her publisher nervous by refusing to reveal even to him where her stories were heading. But she couldn't entirely avoid one of the dominant publication forms of the period.

Her career as a fiction writer began with three short stories labelled *Scenes of Clerical Life*: 'The Sad Fortunes of the Reverend Amos Barton', 'Mr Gilfil's Love-Story', and 'Janet's Repentance', initially published at intervals throughout 1857 in *Blackwood's Edinburgh Magazine* before being gathered in two volumes the following year. Her only periodical novel is *Romola*, serialized at monthly intervals in the *Cornhill Magazine*, for which she briefly parted from her long-time publisher John Blackwood, lured by a large advance. *Middlemarch* and *Daniel Deronda* appeared in stand-alone instalments—every two months for the first six books of *Middlemarch*, then monthly for the remainder and the whole of *Deronda*. She wrote each section far in advance and didn't adapt her work to the format, with its usual contained, digestible portions and cliff-hangers. Once a manuscript was finished, she would quickly leave home for a holiday.

Eliot's 'concept of organic form' extended to style. '[I] have gone through again and again the severe effort of trying to make certain ideas thoroughly incarnate, as if they had revealed themselves to me first in the flesh and not in the spirit' (IV.300), she explained to Frederic Harrison, a jurist who helped her get the legal plot of *Felix Holt* right. Her 'ideal', she emphasized elsewhere, was 'to make matter and form an inseparable truthfulness' (V.374). She appears closer here to a non-fiction writer like Cardinal John Henry Newman, who stated that 'Matter and expression are parts of one: style is a thinking out into language'. For her purposes she needed words and syntax that could think and feel at the same time, conveying meaning but also embodying it.

Eliot knew that such care might count for nothing with readers. Oliver Goldsmith's poem 'Retaliation' satirizes the historian Edmund Burke

> Who, too deep for his hearers, still went on refining,
> And thought of convincing, while they thought of dining;

Eliot reminded her publisher of it, joking that she too was busy 'refining when novel readers only think of skipping' (V.169). Her novels are often classed amongst the 'large loose baggy monsters' Henry James famously accused the Victorians of relentlessly churning out. In classrooms her short novel *Silas Marner* eclipses the rest which, newspaper columnists often worry, are ill suited to an age of distraction. In a 2023 *New Yorker* article announcing 'The End of the English Major', the idea of assigning *Middlemarch* in the era of iPhones is 'like trying to land a 747 on a small rural airstrip'.

Eliot's foothold in popular culture is no stronger than in the classroom. The Premier Inn in Nuneaton describes itself as 'a charming Grade II listed building', and helpfully suggests that it's a useful base from which to visit Shakespeare's home 26 miles away. The blurb doesn't mention an attraction that lies closer still: the hotel is Griff House, where Eliot spent the first 21 years of her life. Unlike the houses of Dickens, Hardy, Gaskell, Carlyle, James, and the Brontës, there is no Eliot museum. Although there have been television adaptations, she hasn't received the Hollywood treatment. She never achieved Dickensian sales nor spawned a Dickensian cultural industry. 'Dickensian' is used inconsistently but pervasively. 'Eliotic' exists too but has never caught on, and is inconveniently shared with the author of *The Waste Land*.

If she has an image at all, it is for being difficult and moral. She can be both. She's surely the most erudite of Victorian novelists: she read seven languages, made important contributions to philosophy, and had a command of physiology, psychology, politics, religious history, and more. Such knowledge, which might have amounted to remoteness, results instead in a plea that we develop more feeling for the people and things around us. This sounds easy. Eliot knew it wasn't. Every perspective was necessary for the enduringly difficult attempt to understand people and, in the process, to sympathize with them. Her novels are absorbing, but in a way that makes a case for the pleasures and value of complexity. As *The Times* wrote shortly after her death, 'Profoundly thoughtful herself, she forced her readers to think in spite of themselves, and nevertheless to read on, instead of throwing her volumes aside.'

Eliot's partner George Henry Lewes nervously wondered whether readers would respond to her vision. She had pitched her first novel, *Adam Bede* (1859), as 'a country story—full of the breath of cows and the scent of hay' (II.387), and its love triangle between an honest carpenter, a naive dairymaid, and the irresponsible local heir sounded promising (Figure 1). However, there was something unusual about her treatment of this age-old tale which gave Lewes pause. He privately recorded his apprehensiveness that readers, in his experience, liked to 'fancy themselves' as the main characters. It didn't seem likely anyone would want to fancy themself an 'upright carpenter who does not rise to be more than a master builder at the end'. Lewes clumsily put his finger on precisely the challenge Eliot hoped readers would be willing to meet: not to identify with characters but to feel for them despite their difference; not to be drawn in by idealized heroes and improbable plots but by the commonplace.

It was a critical triumph. While *Scenes of Clerical Life* had been a pleasant surprise, *Adam Bede* demonstrated that an important new novelist had arrived. *The Times* was clear: 'its author takes rank at once among the masters of the art'. 'It was as good as *going into the country for one's health*' (III.17), raved Jane Carlyle, who urged her friends to read it; Dickens claimed it had 'taken its place among the actual experiences and endurances of my life' (III.114). She was bewildered by a report that Alexandre Dumas considered it 'the greatest novel of the age' (VIII.293). ('After this', she added, 'I will never venture to predict who will like or dislike my books.') On holiday in a remote part of Wales, she overheard people discussing it. A reliable sign of British cultural impact, it was quoted in Parliament: did his opponent, the Liberal MP Charles Buxton asked, wish that his conduct, 'as the farmer's wife said, in *Adam Bede*, could be "hatched over again, and hatched different"'? Initially modest sales leapt up, reaching 16,000 by the end of the year. This was still a long way from the 35,000 Dickens commanded for each part of *Little Dorrit* three years earlier, but it was good.

1. Edward Henry Corbould, *Hetty Sorrel and Captain Donnithorne in Mrs Poyser's dairy* (1861). This is one of two paintings from *Adam Bede* commissioned by Queen Victoria, who loved the novel so much she read it twice in the year it appeared, and felt that Eliot's rural characters resembled the Highlanders she knew well.

Readers waited for Eliot to repeat the success. And waited. They expected more rural charm; Eliot wanted to be free to follow her 'varying unfolding self, and not be a machine always grinding out the same material or spinning the same sort of web' (IV.49). Instead of more hay and dairymaids, she gave them the painfully constricted life of Maggie Tulliver and her family's financial downfall in *The Mill on the Floss* (1860). After the respite of *Silas Marner: The Weaver of Raveloe* (1861), the fable-like tale of a solitary man whose precious hoard of gold is mysteriously swapped for a child, she offered the political and religious machinations of a scrupulously researched 15th-century Florence in *Romola* (1862–3). Either *Adam Bede* hadn't quite been the novel readers had taken it to be or Eliot was changing, and changing fast.

The relief to find her back in the Midlands for *Felix Holt, the Radical* (1866) was short-lived, as readers encountered there an intricate inheritance plot set during a tumultuous parliamentary election. She stayed there to map in *Middlemarch: A Study of Provincial Life* (1871–2) the trajectories of multiple characters as they intersect during their failed bids to fulfil their ambitions. Finally, she ranged across England, Europe, and looked to the Middle East for *Daniel Deronda* (1876), with its parallel accounts of a disastrous marriage and a man's discovery of his Jewish identity and determination to fulfil his visionary friend's dream of a Jewish homeland. By that point, a bewildered reviewer commented, 'it is practically a first book by a new author'.

Eliot's sales mirror her readers' perplexity. Her publishers often lost money punting on the next hit and only *Middlemarch* can be called her other outright popular success, with the cheap edition selling 31,000 copies over a few years. She tried her hand at poetry too, including the long epic poem in five books *The Spanish Gypsy* (1868), set in 15th-century Spain. (As she didn't pull off Thomas Hardy's rare feat of writing poems every bit as magnificent as his novels, the poetry won't feature here.)

Critics nonetheless kept a close eye on her throughout, intrigued—and occasionally annoyed—by the aesthetic and intellectual risks she took, although even after her death many continued to separate the early fiction and later, more demanding, work.

As this book traces, Eliot's fiction did evolve between 1857 and 1876, but often not in the ways her contemporaries imagined. They felt, for example, that her fiction lost its 'charm' as 'anti-Christian feeling grows into a fixed habit with her', ignorant of the fact that she had lost her faith long before writing her first story. Indeed, for all their variety, Eliot's novels present a remarkably cohesive vision. She wanted to test fiction's ability to truly engage with the ordinary, and she wanted to do this to enlarge our capacity for tolerance and generosity. There is nothing naive or sentimental about her request that we be a little more patient, a little more forgiving: her exploration of human psychology, unrivalled in the Victorian novel, reveals a rich understanding of the ways we misread ourselves, each other, and the world. She trusted, though, that exercising our capacity for fellow-feeling would slowly, quietly, change society for the better.

Chapter 1
Gossip

On 2 January 1842 Robert Evans, the High Anglican retired manager of the Arbury estate in Warwickshire, recorded his daughter's aberrant behaviour in his diary: 'Went to Trinity Church in the forenoon. Miss Lewis went with me. Mary Ann did not go.' This was the pivotal moment in what George Eliot—then Mary Ann Evans—referred to as her '"Holy War"' (I.133). Following a second refusal to attend church, she left home to stay with her brother Isaac, 'excommunicated' in 'compliance with my Father's wish that I should retire for a time from a neighbourhood in which I had been placed on the very comfortable pedestal of the town gazing-stock' (I.137–8).

With all the proud idealism of a 22-year-old, Eliot continued in the same letter that her father 'could not place a more effective barrier to my "conversion" than by making my apparent worldly interests in any way dependent on it'. If she yielded, it wouldn't be on account of 'the good opinion of the world'. The explanation she dispatched to her father was only slightly less bullish. Her stance was not based on an allegiance with one Christian denomination over another: having come to regard scripture as 'histories consisting of mingled truth and fiction', she no longer identified with any. More outrageous still, while she could 'admire and cherish much of what I believe to have been the moral teaching of Jesus himself', the 'system of doctrines' that had been built on his life was 'pernicious in its influence on individual and social happiness'. She could not, then, 'without vile hypocrisy and a miserable truckling to the smile of the world for the sake of my supposed interests, profess to join in worship which I wholly disapprove' (I.128–9).

Eliot had been revising her views on scripture for some time, but to her family the change must have seemed like a volte-face. Since becoming close to Maria Lewis, a governess at her boarding school, Eliot's teenage evangelical fervour had seen her abjure theatre trips, secular music ('it would not cost me any regrets if the only music heard in our land were that of strict worship', I.13), and novels ('I shall carry to my grave the mental diseases with which they have contaminated me', I.22). In the full throes of the kind of renunciation practised in *The Mill on the Floss* by Maggie Tulliver, who turns her mirror to face the wall, she 'used to go about like an owl', much to her brother's irritation.

There had been signs, though, that she was becoming less entrenched—an anxious sense that she needed 'melting and remoulding' (I.48), a hysteric outburst at a party, and a richer literary diet that included Romantic poetry, historical biblical criticism, and science. Her introduction in November 1841 to the intellectually curious and freethinking Bray family brought matters to a head. Almost immediately, she confided to her erstwhile religious confidante Maria: 'My whole soul has been engrossed in the most interesting of all enquiries for the last few days, and to what result my thoughts may lead I know not—possibly to one that will startle you' (I.120). And so, two months later, Eliot did not go to church.

Although Eliot's break with Christianity influenced how she has been perceived ever since, what happened next may have had as much impact on her work and self-representation: she went back. The compromise she reached with her father ('the one deep strong love I have ever known' (I.284), she later wrote in 1849 as he was dying) was that she would accompany him to church but would be entitled to think as she pleased. The crisis over, within two months she regretted her 'impetuosity both of feeling and judging' (I.134). Nearly 30 years later, a friend revealed, Eliot still dwelt on 'how much fault there is on the side of the young in such cases, of their ignorance of life, & the narrowness of their intellectual superiority'. The episode had taught her lessons—about independence, family ties, social pressure, compromise, and self-checking—that she would carry throughout her life.

Sexual scandals

The 'Holy War' unfolded on a domestic and local scale; the sexual scandals in which she became embroiled were far more public. Eliot was acutely conscious of her lack of beauty, which so many later described—'magnificently ugly—deliciously hideous', with 'a vast pendulous nose' and 'a mouth with huge protruding "English" teeth' redeemed, everyone agreed, by a captivating voice. This, combined with her unusual intellectual powers, fuelled the painful belief that she would never find love: aged 20, she concluded prematurely that 'Every day's experience seems to deepen the voice of foreboding that has long been telling me, "The bliss of reciprocated affection is not allotted to you under any form"' (I.70). Characters in Eliot's novels who predict the future are usually proved wrong, and she was proved wrong too.

As her Coventry circle of friends expanded, so did opportunities—she took on translation work and began reviewing for provincial and then national publications—and with these came romantic possibility. She flirted with an artist. A visit with the 62-year-old scholar Dr Brabant during which she was 'petted and fed with nice morsels and pretty speeches' (I.166) was curtailed when Mrs Brabant took exception to the petting. History repeated itself when, nearly 18 months after the death of her father, Eliot began lodging with the publisher John Chapman at 142 Strand, London, provoking the jealousy of both his wife and mistress. (Eliot became indispensable as the unofficial editor of Chapman's *Westminster Review*, however, and so accommodation—literal and emotional—was found.) She developed stronger feelings for the philosopher-scientist Herbert Spencer who, unable to reciprocate, began bringing along a friend. This was George Henry Lewes.

The vivacious polymath with whom Eliot came to share nearly 25 years of her life was a cosmopolitan, largely self-educated man of letters who enjoyed amateur theatrics with Dickens, wrote bad novels and good articles, and later gained respect for his biography of Goethe and his physiological research. Nicknamed 'the Ape' by the Carlyles, Lewes was a provocateur who once alarmed Charlotte Brontë by insisting they had 'both written naughty books'. He also happened to be married. Lewes had five children with his wife Agnes (three survived), who also had four children with Lewes's married friend Thornton Leigh Hunt. Lewes and Eliot met in October 1851; by March 1853, she admitted that he 'has quite won my liking, in spite of myself' (II.94); by April, she saw 'a man of heart and conscience wearing a mask of flippancy' (II.98). On 20 July 1854, the 34-year-old Eliot and the 37-year-old Lewes left together for Germany.

This time, there was no turning back. Unlike Maggie Tulliver, who semi-consciously drifts on the river Floss into an elopement with a man unworthy of the sacrifice, Eliot had made a careful and considered choice. She wrote to John Chapman:

> I do not wish to take the ground of ignoring what is unconventional in my position. I have counted the cost of the step that I have taken and am prepared to bear, without irritation or bitterness, renunciation by all my friends. I am not mistaken in the person to whom I have attached myself. He is worthy of the sacrifice I have incurred, and my only anxiety is that he should be rightly judged. (VIII.124–5)

Even if the path to divorce had been easier then (the Matrimonial Causes Act only came into law in 1857), Lewes and Eliot would likely have shied from the publicity of taking it. But there was little they could do to stem the gossip that quickly spread.

Eliot did not lose all her friends, but she did lose some, and the couple lost sleep over the difficult letters they received. A phrenological reading of Eliot's skull had once promised that her 'moral' region was 'quite sufficient to keep the animal in order', but the horrified phrenologist George Combe now wondered whether insanity lurked among her ancestors. She also lost family: having ascertained in 1857 that she was not legally 'Mrs. Lewes', Isaac cut ties with her and urged their sister Chrissey and half-sister Fanny to do the same. On her deathbed two years later, Chrissey broke her silence in a letter full of regret at having given in to their domineering brother. Despite the heavy price she paid, Eliot's union with Lewes was by all accounts remarkably happy; Eliot felt she had 'begun life afresh' (II.170), and the rich emotional and intellectual companionship she had finally found undoubtedly played a part in her transition from journalism to the novels that made (in every way) her name.

Her exposure to sexual scandals was not over. Seven months before her death from kidney disease in 1880, the 60-year-old Eliot raised eyebrows once more by marrying the 40-year-old banker John Walter Cross. Lewes had died 18 months earlier and a distraught Eliot found solace in the friend who was himself grieving the recent death of his mother. As if the age gap was not matter enough for gossip, during their honeymoon in Venice Cross threw himself into the Canal, amplifying speculations about a marriage too brief to be readily understood. Rigidly following propriety to the last, Isaac ended an estrangement of 23 years by sending his sister a formal note of congratulations on the 'happy event' (VII.280). Eliot, with greater warmth, wrote back that 'our long silence has never broken the affection for you which began when we were little ones' (VII.287). She died shortly afterwards, leaving her widower to tell the world the story of George Eliot.

'George Eliot'

George Eliot came into the world on 4 February 1857. Cross explained that when she opted to publish her fiction pseudonymously, 'the reason she fixed on this name was that George was Mr Lewes's Christian name, and Eliot was a good mouth-filling, easily-pronounced word'. The pseudonym proved a stable identity for the novelist, who had no such fixed name in her own life. She was born Mary Anne Evans on 22 November 1819, played with the name Marianne Evans in her homework, signed her sister's marriage register Mary Ann Evans, and was Marian Evans for her translation *The Essence of Christianity*.

There were more. In short pieces for the *Pall Mall Gazette* she is 'Saccharissa'. She was 'Clematis' to some childhood friends and Pollian (a pun on Apollyon) to others. She was 'Mrs Lewes' for nosy landladies, asked friends to refer to her as Marian Evans Lewes, and was, briefly, legally Mary Ann Evans Lewes in order to wrap up her financial affairs after Lewes's death; she died Mary Ann Cross on 22 December 1880. She was often Polly to Lewes, and 'Beatrice' (after Dante's unrequited love) to Cross. When she launched her fiction career in *Blackwood's Edinburgh Magazine*, her three stories appeared anonymously. 'George Eliot' was first tested in a letter to her publisher William Blackwood and then publicly appended to the book publication of *Scenes of Clerical Life* in 1858. Why has 'George Eliot' stuck whereas Currer, Ellis, and Acton Bell have reverted to Charlotte, Emily, and Anne Brontë? Perhaps because it is far from clear which name we should revert to.

If Eliot wanted a pseudonym in part so she would be judged as a novelist rather than as a female novelist, then this wouldn't have been unreasonable. In 18th-century French culture, she argued in her 1854 article 'Woman in France', there was no need for women to prove they 'could write as well as men'. That she could expect the same in 19th-century England was put into doubt when, having discovered who 'George Eliot' really was, the *Saturday Review* recalled how critics were wrong-footed: *Adam Bede* had been thought 'too good for a woman's story'. (Not for Dickens, who congratulated himself on having detected 'womanly touches', II.424.) Now that the author of *The Mill on the Floss* was known to be a woman, was it 'quite consistent with feminine delicacy to lay so much stress on the bodily feelings of the other sex'? Indeed, should Eliot have described the sensation 'raised in a man's mind by gazing at a woman's arm'? The reviewer thought not.

Yet the opprobrium facing Victorian female novelists shouldn't be exaggerated. The Poet Laureate Robert Southey's warning to Charlotte Brontë in 1837 that 'Literature cannot be the business of a woman's life: & it ought not to be' would have sounded quaint to many mid-century ears. That the author of *Scenes of Clerical Life* and *Adam Bede* was this particular woman was more germane. The fact evidently tested Elizabeth Gaskell's considerable powers of tolerance: she wrote Eliot a fan letter full of praise, but admitted: 'I wish you *were Mrs.* Lewes. However that can't be helped, as far as I can see, and one must not judge others.' The revelation sent others, still warm from the glow of *Adam Bede*'s benevolently moral narrator, into a state of profound confusion: 'Such a fact destroys all comfortable notions of right and wrong, true and false, as they make the writer quite independent of personal character.'

But gender was only part of the reason for choosing a pseudonym: another was Eliot's knowledge of the literary marketplace and canny awareness 'that a *nom de plume* secures all the advantages without the disagreeables of reputation' (II.292). Certainly, not all gossip was harmful. She also foresaw that if her turn to fiction proved unsuccessful and 'George Eliot' be deemed 'an ineffective writer—a mere flash in the pan—I, for one, am determined to cut him on the first intimation of that disagreeable fact' (II.309–10). She urged Blackwood to hasten the publication of *Adam Bede* before her mask was torn off.

Anonymity (or pseudonymity) may have afforded 'the highest *prestige*' (II.309), but it also brought trouble. While fun could be had hearing oneself praised incognito, it was inconvenient not to be able to openly take credit when someone like Dickens was eager to know more about the author. It was harder still when others were given, or simply took, that credit. The well-established novelists Edward Bulwer-Lytton and Elizabeth Gaskell were mooted as possible solutions to the mystery of 'George Eliot', but the name that stuck was altogether less glamorous: Liggins.

Eliot's half-sister Fanny, having been left in the dark, began openly speculating that the Nuneaton-raised failed clergyman Joseph Liggins was the author of *Scenes of Clerical Life*, a conjecture which, shared by other locals, found its way into the press. An initially entertaining confusion became embarrassing. Journalists eager to smoke out the trending author piled on, assuming outrage at the obfuscation: such 'concealments' were 'a species of literary fraud' (III.62 n.), decried the *Leader*; the *Athenaeum* couldn't see why such 'mystification' was necessary. The speculation lasted for some months after the publication of *Adam Bede*, but Eliot gave in to pressure in the summer of 1859: the veil was lifted. 'Brother Jacob', a little-read short story written the following year, has often been interpreted as an oblique commentary on these events: it is about a man who takes on a fake name to begin a new life, but whose cover is blown by inconvenient family relations. Eliot had learnt one more lesson about being the centre of idle, and sometimes mischievous, talk.

Gossip

'This world', *Middlemarch* states, is 'a huge whispering-gallery'. Few novelists wrote better, or more frequently, about gossip than George Eliot. Gossip defines the boundaries of her characters' universe: she jokes that Mr Brooke is 'brave enough to defy the world—that is to say, Mrs Cadwallader the Rector's wife, and the small group of gentry with whom he visited in the north-east corner of Loamshire'. It acts as a social glue, a kind of provincial theatre in which participants rehearse familiar roles.

Gossip is not necessarily malicious. *OED* definitions range from 'easy, unrestrained talk' about 'persons or social incidents' to 'trifling or groundless rumour'. Eliot was exceptionally good at dialogue, occasionally jotting down in her journal expressions that caught her ear. The long set pieces she became famous for, in which she appears to transcribe, unobserved, a group in full flow—tea parties, family conclaves, pub scenes—show a relish for capturing the rhythms and comic energy of speech. Witness Mrs Pullet savouring her neighbours' ailments: '"I've seen her legs when they was like bladders"'.

Eliot draws on gossip for the form as well as the content of her fiction. We are eavesdropping too, she makes clear in *Scenes of Clerical Life*, and 'now that we are snug and warm with this little tea-party', 'we will listen to what they are talking about'; the conversations in *Adam Bede* are 'overheard' by readers. The narrators of these early works also claim to have picked up information from other characters: 'But I gathered from Adam Bede, to whom I talked of these matters in his old age, that few clergymen could be less successful in winning the hearts of their parishioners than Mr Ryde.'

But gossip is also how society ensures conformity and punishes transgressions. Financial scandal, the shame of insolvency, and outright theft run through the fiction, and with it dishonour. Sexual scandal is worse. Extramarital relations—Hetty and Arthur in *Adam Bede*, Tito Melema and Tessa in *Romola*, Mrs Transome and Matthew Jermyn in *Felix Holt*—wreak havoc, but the damage caused by unfounded rumours is often as bad. Amos Barton's misguided but innocent loyalty to the sponging Countess Czerlaski causes irreparable harm. Maggie's choice not to go through with her elopement with Stephen Guest leaves her in such a social limbo that the novel sees no other solution but to kill her off. Suspicions regarding the refuge Reverend Rufus Lyon offers to Annette lead him to resign the ministry. Grandcourt uses the threat of what society will say to control Gwendolen's relations with Daniel Deronda. When rumours about his sister reach Tom Tulliver's ears, he expects 'the worst': 'not death, but disgrace'.

There is more to gossip than ostracism. It also taps into Eliot's concern with how little we know of each other and ourselves. Years of having been misrepresented herself no doubt played its part. She was adamant that 'there is not a *single person* who is in a position to make a true representation' (II.196) of her relationship with Lewes. In *Scenes of Clerical Life*, she pondered how 'Our daily familiar life is but a hiding of ourselves from each other behind a screen of trivial words and deeds'. Watching the astonishment on the faces of friends to whom she confessed she was the author of *Adam Bede* further increased her conception of 'the ignorance in which we all live of each other'.

Her feelings about this were ambivalent. She could treat it as a joke: 'Thank heaven', she exclaims in *Scenes of Clerical Life*, 'that we don't know exactly what our friends think of us'. But it's given a darker, gothic treatment in her novella *The Lifted Veil* (1859), in which the narrator Latimer is subjected to precisely that torture: he is endowed with the supernatural gift of hearing people's thoughts. Eliot's natural bent was also one of privacy rather than confession. She frequently hurt close friends by failing to confide in them, leaving them to discover the most momentous events of her life—her relationships, her authorship—second-hand. Even so, such secrecy comes at a cost, in the novels as in life. The central protagonist of *Daniel Deronda* carries a precarious sense of self built, for much of the novel, on false rumours about his identity, and the work offers her most sustained attack on the psychological, interpersonal, and even cultural damage wrought by concealment.

Eliot instinctively shrank from both display and misinterpretation, and fantasized about people being loved not because they are fully exposed, but despite remaining hidden. Mr Gilfil states:

> God sees us as we are altogether, not in separate feelings or action, as our fellow-men see us. We are always doing each other injustice, and thinking better or worse of each other than we deserve, because we only hear and see separate words and actions. We don't see each other's whole nature.

Narrators can be God-like in their omniscience, but people can't. Knowing others' circumstances—as much as neighbours can know of each other—ought to be enough to bring out the best in us, as it does for Janet Dempster and Silas Marner once their community, discovering their troubles, stops idly speculating about them. It shouldn't rely on the delusion that we can read people like an open book. Still new to the rumour-mill surrounding celebrities, Eliot privately expressed her desire to 'write something that would contribute to heighten men's reverence before the secrets of each other's souls, that there might be less assumption of entire knowingness' (III.164).

That's the ideal. In practice, Eliot knew that gossip is a fact of life that can't be wished away. It shapes how we come to think about ourselves, and an over-reliance on the world's good opinion of us can lull us into thinking we are incapable of serious harm, as it does Arthur Donnithorne. The world is also able to sense truths about ourselves we don't suspect. Eliot's eccentric final work

Impressions of Theophrastus Such (1879) consists largely of character sketches that dramatize the gap between our social identity and self-impressions. '[W]hile there are secrets in me unguessed by others', the narrator proposes, 'these others have certain items of knowledge about the extent of my powers and the figure I make with them, which in turn are secrets unguessed by me.' Gossip can wound and distort, but it often contains a kernel of truth.

We are social animals and, as such, are not masters of our destiny: this is one of Eliot's central themes. She liked representing a stranger joining a close-knit community—Edgar Tryan settling in Milby, Silas Marner in Raveloe, 'David Faux' in Grimworth, Tertius Lydgate in Middlemarch, Henleigh Mallinger Grandcourt in Diplow—and tracing the impact of an individual on a community and of a community on an individual. The ambitious doctor Lydgate intends to 'do good small work for Middlemarch, and great work for the world', and to achieve this on his own terms. Middlemarch has other ideas and 'counted on swallowing Lydgate and assimilating him very comfortably'. Middlemarch wins (Figure 2).

Fantasies of independence are shown to be precisely that: 'For there is no creature whose inward being is so strong that it is not greatly determined by what lies outside it.' A reviewer of *Middlemarch* was struck by this sentence, rightly noting that 'it sounds at the first hearing like a truism, but it is a truism to which George Eliot's genius has restored all the vividness of a truth'. We deplore the petty provincial conformity that clips Lydgate's wings, but Eliot's complex treatment of the theme is such that she is also able to give provincial conformity a fair hearing. Strict adherence to principles, after all, is what leads aunt Glegg to offer her slandered niece Maggie Tulliver a shelter.

Making one's peace with idle talk was easier said than done. Lewes quickly discovered that the slightest critique or clumsy comment about her fiction threw Eliot into a state of debilitating

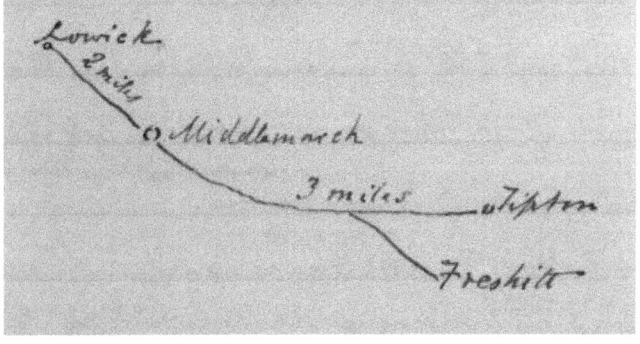

2. Eliot's preparations for *Middlemarch* included working out the various ways in which her characters were linked, geographically and personally. 'Quarry for Middlemarch', MS Lowell 13, Houghton Library, Harvard University.

dejection. He began acting as her filter to the world, inspecting her letters beforehand, hiding negative reviews (she often came across them anyway), and urging visitors to be careful. 'This between ourselves. When you see her, mind your care is to discountenance the idea of a Romance being the product of an Encyclopædia' (III.474), he enjoined Blackwood as Eliot sank into a seemingly bottomless pit of research for *Romola*.

Eliot's jealous rival novelist Margaret Oliphant envied the 'mental greenhouse' Lewes built for her, which she felt had allowed her genius to grow. Might she too have achieved greater things in more congenial circumstances? Would Lydgate have changed world medicine if he had not met Rosamond or become embroiled with Bulstrode? Eliot could have pointedly directed Oliphant to a passage in *Middlemarch*: 'It always remains true that if we had been greater, circumstance would have been less strong against us.'

Life-writing

Eliot wrote in 1859 that her books had 'come out of all the painful discipline, all the most hardly-learnt lessons of my past life' (III.187). Growing up a preternaturally clever girl in early 19th-century provincial Warwickshire couldn't have been easy—'when she was young', she later confided, 'girls and women seemed to look on her as somehow "uncanny"'—nor could the later experience of becoming an outcast. Her feelings appear at their most raw in *The Mill on the Floss*. It's her most autobiographical novel, drawing on memories of her aunts; the trials of having cared for an ailing father; of reading Thomas à Kempis to sustain herself; of her strong childhood affection for her brother Isaac, from whom she received so much severity; and of social ostracism—all reworked into an account of Maggie's frustrated yearning for love so poignant that it made Proust cry.

Men who visited the 'Leweses' in England didn't bring their wives. In the novel, the 'ladies of St Ogg's' bear the brunt of Eliot's bitterness: 'Public opinion, in these cases, is always of the feminine gender—not the world, but the world's wife.' It is 'the ladies' who indulge in their 'favourite abstraction, called Society, which served to make their consciences perfectly easy in doing what satisfied their own egoism—thinking and speaking the worst of Maggie Tulliver, and turning their backs upon her'. Meanwhile, the men joke, shrugging their shoulders 'at the mutual hatred of women'. Eliot's critics have often similarly smiled at the way her wide-reaching sympathy tends to wobble when representing fashionable women, usually blonde.

Eliot insisted in 1861 that 'It was never a trial to me to have been cut off from what is called the world, and I think I love none of my fellow-creatures the less for it' (III.396). But critics have often regretted the effects of what Henry James called 'sequestration' on her novels: 'If her relations with the world had been easier', he believed, 'her books would have been less difficult'. In a 1919 essay, Virginia Woolf felt that the charm surrounding the young Maggie Tulliver disappears when Eliot has a 'full-grown woman on her hands' who must interact with society—a society in which the novelist felt 'out of her element'. The humour vanishes, the satire becomes clunky, and what remains is 'the vindictiveness of a grudge which we feel to be personal in its origin'.

The first reviewers of *Middlemarch* had further evidence that she never quite resolved her complicated feelings about what she described in that novel as the 'hampering threadlike pressure of small social conditions'. Like Lydgate, Dorothea Brooke's ardent idealism is stifled by a badly misjudged marriage, hers to the hyper-sensitive, desiccated scholar Casaubon. 'Such mistakes could not have happened', Eliot concluded the first edition of the novel, 'if the society into which she was born had not smiled on propositions of marriage from a sickly man to a girl less than half his own age'. Reviewers cried foul: Middlemarch society had very much *not* smiled on Casaubon's proposition. 'What more could Dorothea's friends have done unless they had put strychnine in Casaubon's tea?', one exasperated critic asked. Finding the objection fair, Eliot dropped the passage from later editions, but the slip was revealing.

Once out of provincial England and well on her way in literary London, Eliot shuddered to think of returning to live with her sister: to be 'in that hideous neighbourhood amongst ignorant bigots is impossible to me. It would be moral asphyxia and I had better take the other kind' (II.97). The harshness may surprise those used to the wide tolerance of her narrators. Looking back over a rich career rather than at its threshold, she later struck a different note. In a beautiful passage from *Impressions of Theophrastus Such*, the semi-autobiographical narrator accepts that, having long departed from the provincial England of his youth, 'now my consciousness is chiefly of the busy, anxious metropolitan sort'. And yet. 'There have been many voluntary exiles in the world', she writes, and

> some of those who sallied forth went for the sake of a loved companionship, when they would willingly have kept sight of the familiar plains, and of the hills to which they had first lifted up their eyes.

Because of course Eliot did return to Warwickshire—in her fiction. The 'childish loves', the 'memory of that warm little nest where my affections were fledged', as Theophrastus writes, animated her, and it is with such familiar places in mind that she began to write fiction.

Scenes of Clerical Life felt 'familiar' to others too, and readers were spurred to match fictional characters and locations to real ones. Milby 'was' Nuneaton, Shepperton Church 'was' Chilvers Coton parish church, and Arbury Hall 'was' Cheverel Manor; the Reverend Bernard Gilpin Ebdell was surely Mr Gilfil, the Newdigates were no doubt the Cheverels. Others thought they'd recognized themselves: the Reverend John Gwyther put himself forward as the original Amos Barton and found it 'unkind and taking a great liberty with a living Character' (III.84). The Reverend W. P. Jones, having identified the Reverend Tryan as his dead brother, was 'utterly at a loss to conceive who could have written the statements or revived what should have been buried in oblivion' (II.375).

Eliot was rattled. There was some truth to the claims. 'Janet's Repentance' was a 'real bit in the religious history of England that happened about eight-and-twenty years ago', when an evangelical clergyman very much like Tryan was subjected to 'vicious' 'persecution' by the community (II.347). She insisted to Blackwood, though, that Tryan 'is not a portrait of any clergyman, living or dead' (II.375). To be sure, there were '*two* portraits in the Clerical Scenes', she admitted, 'but that was my first bit of art, and my hand was not well in' (III.99). Like any artist, Eliot reserved the right to transmute her sources of inspiration as she saw fit: 'I should consider it a fault which would cause me lasting regret, if I had used reality in any other than the legitimate way common to all artists who draw their materials from their observation and experience' (II.376).

Clearly it would not do, Eliot saw, to make familiar materials too familiar. Art, she wrote loftily to Blackwood, is made from 'a combination of subtle shadowy suggestions with certain actual objects and events', but when 'people discover certain points of coincidence in a fiction with facts that happen to have come to their knowledge, they believe themselves able to furnish a key to the whole' (II.459). She continued to write '"out of my own life"' (III.129)—*Adam Bede*'s Methodist preacher Dinah Morris draws on memories of her aunt, and Adam Bede himself of her father, and she even took the name of the schoolteacher Bartle Massey from her father's childhood teacher—but she would henceforth be more careful.

Nevertheless, Eliot was a novelist who did need to anchor her fiction in the real world. Her preparations for her novels involved extensive research, both inside the study and out of it. She based the weather depicted in *Adam Bede* on meteorological records from the period when the novel is set; the flood at the end of *The Mill on the Floss* is drawn from a real flood. Like a painter, she sought models outdoors, touring Dorset with Lewes in quest of a good mill for her novel and location-scouting grand houses in Wiltshire for *Daniel Deronda*. Why, one might wonder, didn't she simply make them up? The answer lies somewhere in her aesthetic and ethical commitment to the real.

Chapter 2
Realism

What do we see when we look? The Victorian art critic John Ruskin set his readers an exercise:

> Take the commonest, closest, most familiar thing, and strive to draw it verily as you see it. Be sure of this last fact, for otherwise you will find yourself continually drawing, not what you *see*, but what you *know*. The best practice to begin with is, sitting about three yards from a bookcase (not your own, so that you may *know* none of the titles of the books), to try to draw the books accurately, with the titles on the backs, and patterns on the bindings, as you see them. You are not to stir from your place to look what they are, but to draw them simply as they appear, giving the perfect look of neat lettering; which, nevertheless, must be (as you find it on most of the books) absolutely illegible.

George Eliot shared Ruskin's curiosity about the nature of observation. Like him, she knew that we see and therefore represent the world through the lens of our personalities, expectations, and the conventions of the period in which we live. She also knew that genuine observation could yield surprising results. Her fiction is a riposte to those she described in an essay as treating 'their subjects under the influence of traditions and prepossessions rather than of direct observation'.

The Victorian period is considered the apogee of literary realism and George Eliot its high priestess, even though she rarely used the word 'realism'. When she did, it was mostly in relation to Ruskin, whom she judged, in the mid-1850s, 'the finest writer living' (II.255). Her review of Ruskin's *Modern Painters* glossed the new-fangled term. Realism was:

> the doctrine that all truth and beauty are to be attained by a humble and faithful study of nature, and not by substituting vague forms, bred by imagination on the mists of feeling, in place of definite, substantial reality.

The word had originally been used in late 18th-century philosophy to refer to external objects that exist independently of the mind, and now addressed questions of artistic representation.

This and other essays Eliot wrote for the *Westminster Review* around that time are often read as attempts to formulate, for herself as much as others, her own 'doctrine'—the theory before the practice. Visual arts continued to provide a useful reference point. One of her best-known pieces, 'The Natural History of German Life' (1856), is a long review-essay of a sociological study by Wilhelm Heinrich von Riehl. Having praised Riehl's scrupulous account, she asks: 'Where, in our picture exhibitions, shall we find a group of true peasantry?' By looking 'for its subjects into literature instead of life', artists had heaped cliché on cliché: 'buxom' cottage matrons, 'joyous' labourers cracking jokes, and 'idyllic swains and damsels' posing like 'chimney ornaments'. One had only to see William Holman Hunt's painting *The Hireling Shepherd* to be struck by the contrast between his carefully rendered landscape and improbable pastoral lovers (Figure 3).

Eliot found that she couldn't, in fact, wholly shake off theorizing once she left off articles for fiction. The narrator of

3. William Holman Hunt, *The Hireling Shepherd* (1851–2).

Adam Bede often sounds very much like the reviewer of the
Westminster. He tells us (Eliot's early narrators are male) that his
'bucolic' characters are 'not of that entirely genial, merry,
broad-grinning sort, apparently observed in most districts
visited by artists'. The much analysed chapter 17, titled 'In Which
the Story Pauses a Little', is largely given over to what might
fairly be called a manifesto in defence of 'the faithful
representing of commonplace things'. Seventeenth-century
Dutch paintings gave her a model to work with in terms of their
'faithful pictures of a monotonous homely existence' (Figure 4).
Here were painters willing to show 'old women scraping carrots
with their work-worn hands', or 'an old woman bending over her
flower-pot'.

This was all very well, but even the boldest of experimental
novelists might pale at the thought of writing 215,000 words
(roughly the length of *Adam Bede*) about old women scraping
carrots. Throughout her career, Eliot experimented with the
extent to which fiction might accommodate the ordinary.

4. Eliot saw Gerrit Dou's 17th-century painting *The Prayer of the Spinner* while visiting Munich in 1858.

Falsism

In many ways, it was easier for Eliot to clarify what literary realism wasn't. Realism, she explained in *Adam Bede*, shouldn't try to 'make things seem better than they were'. But realism wasn't copyism either. Reviewers sometimes misunderstood this and objected to fiction being used as 'a series of photographic studies', as if such a thing were even possible. A realist novelist was also entitled to make use of all manner of creative freedoms, as George Henry Lewes made clear in a distinction that also underpins Eliot's fiction. The antithesis of realism wasn't idealism, he wrote, but '*Falsism*'. Similarly, the narrator of

Adam Bede is 'content to tell my simple story...dreading nothing, indeed, but falsity'.

That Eliot reached more frequently for the words 'true' and 'false' than 'realism' to account for her aims implies a flexible understanding of what the novelist might do. Another word she relied on was 'sincere'. Objectivity was impossible. What was required was truth of perception, in other words representations that were 'faithful' insofar as they showed things 'as they have mirrored themselves in my mind'. Consequently, as she argued in another essay, the 'fantastic or the boldly imaginative poet may be as sincere as the most realistic' so long as he is 'true to his own sensibilities or inward vision'. In fact, it was often when an obsession with getting things factually right triumphed over a more artistic concept of truthfulness—15th-century Florence, say, or the history of Jewish mysticism—that she got into trouble.

In 'The Natural History of German Life', Eliot tried her hand at a 'faithful' description of English peasants:

> But no one who has seen much of actual ploughmen thinks them jocund; no one who is well acquainted with the English peasantry can pronounce them merry. The slow gaze, in which no sense of beauty beams, no humour twinkles,—the slow utterance, and the heavy, slouching walk, remind one rather of that melancholy animal the camel than of the sturdy countryman, with striped stockings, red waistcoat, and hat aside, who represents the traditional English peasant.

A camel? This is no longer sociology, but something else entirely. The cliché of the 'traditional' peasant has been replaced with something unexpected, just as Ruskin's student artist might be surprised to realize afresh how a bookshelf looks from a distance. Surprise is important: for Eliot, a 'picture of human life such as a great artist can give, surprises even the trivial and the selfish into that attention to what is apart from themselves'. Camels are not intrinsically melancholy; the adjective reminds us that any exercise in attentiveness is inevitably shaped by the perceiving mind. (Eliot had the chance to test the comparison: she regularly visited the Zoological Gardens, now London Zoo, whose Camel House opened in the 1830s.) This is hardly realism as a 'slavishly literal rendering', as one of Eliot's reviewers complained. No wonder one of her ardent admirers was Vincent Van Gogh.

Novelists were as guilty of falsification as painters. Eliot's acerbic essay 'Silly Novels by Lady Novelists' (1856) shows her in full satirical swing as she pulls apart the inanities of third-rate contemporary novelists. She invents categories for their paltry efforts, such as the '*mind-and-millinery* species' in which the heroine's 'nose and her morals are alike free from any tendency to irregularity', who 'dances like a sylph, and reads the Bible in the original tongues'. These were novels in which good people were good-looking, villains were ugly, and 4-year-olds sounded like bad poets. Like George Orwell in his attack on stale imagery in 'Politics and the English Language', Eliot again excoriated cliché—novels in which 'the lover has a manly breast; minds are redolent of various things; hearts are hollow; events are utilized; friends are consigned to the tomb . . .'.

Bad writing was also bad morality. Reviewing the novel *Constance Herbert*, Eliot was angered by how Geraldine Jewsbury sought to enforce the principle of an 'uncompromising sacrifice of inclination to duty' in a manner that disproportionately rewarded the renouncer who, it turned out, hadn't sacrificed much at all. This was 'copy-book morality', false both to the nature of renunciation and to 'the realities of life'. If renunciation was so painless, Eliot argued, it would not be 'moral heroism' but simply 'a calculation of prudence'. Maggie Tulliver is in many ways Eliot's rebuttal to Jewsbury: nothing about Maggie's renunciations is painless.

'The notion that duty looks stern, but all the while has her hand full of sugar-plums, with which she will reward us by-and-by, is the favourite cant of optimists.' In another article, Eliot launched an attack on 'the so-called moral *dénouement*, in which rewards and punishments are distributed' according to dubious and unrealistic 'notions of justice'. What sentiments were really being gratified, she wondered, in the pleasure readers took in seeing a villain 'crushed by a railway train'? Eliot's novels contain no villains; her endings are often bittersweet. She told her publisher that the 'moral effect' of her stories depended on her 'power of seeing truly and feeling justly' (II.362). For her the two were inseparable.

Common people

Eliot's realism began as an aesthetic and moral fidelity to the representation of 'commonplace people'. In her early works—*Scenes of Clerical Life, Adam Bede, The Mill on the Floss*, and *Silas Marner*—'commonplace' meant largely the rural and provincial lower classes. (Not exclusively. Interactions with wealthier people are central to the plots.) 'The Natural History of German Life' had made a case for the important work to be done in this area: she was conscious of how 'little the real characteristics of the working-classes are known to those who are outside them'. The stakes were higher here than correcting misrepresentations about 'the manners and conversation of beaux and duchesses': 'Falsification here is far more pernicious'.

Eliot wasn't 'slumming it'. She avoided extreme destitution—she didn't follow Dickens into London rookeries, Gaskell into Manchester slums, or Condition of England novelists into factories. Her early protagonists (like those of her first story, 'neither in rags nor in velvet') are struggling curates, carpenters, modest tenant farmers. Nor had she made the mistake, as one periodical remarked approvingly, of those novelists who, 'writing about things with which they can have but a very imperfect acquaintance', produced a 'stage view' of the 'lower classes' no more authentic than Marie-Antoinette's infamous shepherdess costumes. Here was 'the genuine article'.

It was 'genuine' partly because it came from observation. Eliot's mother was a farmer's daughter and her father was a carpenter's son who worked up to become manager of the 7,000-acre Arbury estate. As a child, she often accompanied him and came to know the grand ancestral hall (she had access to its library), the poor cottagers living on the estate, and the mining community nearby. The large red-brick farmhouse in which she grew up included stables and a dairy. Later, a rumour circulated that, after her mother's death from breast cancer when Eliot was 16, she worked in the dairy, crushing the curd like Hetty Sorrel, which led to her right hand becoming larger than her left. (Isaac Evans's family, always hyper-conscious about respectability, stiffly insisted that Eliot 'never touched a cheese'.)

She had non-autobiographical models too. It's hard to imagine there could have been a George Eliot without there having first been a William Wordsworth. Over half a century earlier, Wordsworth had set out to write poems 'to shew that men who do not wear fine cloaths can feel deeply'. Eliot retained her first impression, on her 20th birthday, of having 'never before met with so many of my own feelings, expressed just as I could like them' (I.34) as in his poetry. (A red flag is raised in the novels whenever a character doesn't like *Lyrical Ballads*.) He encountered on the 'public road' the 'passions of mankind' found in 'Souls that appear to have no depth at all | To vulgar eyes'. She wanted to shine a light on the passions of 'insignificant people, whom you pass unnoticingly on the road every day', as she claims in *The Mill on the Floss*. The epigraph of *Adam Bede* is taken from Wordsworth, as is that for *Silas Marner*—a novel for which she considered Wordsworth her ideal reader.

What had been done in poetry was new to novels. She saw this: the early works can be defensive, sometimes clumsily so.

'[P]erhaps I am doing a bold thing to bespeak your sympathy on behalf of a man who was so very far from remarkable', she writes in *Scenes of Clerical Life*; 'I am not ashamed of commemorating old Kester', she interjects in *Adam Bede*; faced with 'sordid' lives, readers of *The Mill on the Floss* were probably 'irritated with these dull men and women'.

Many readers responded powerfully to what they agreed was a new element in literature. Her work, they said, was 'so true, and so natural'. Unlike Dickens's 'preternaturally virtuous poor children', as Eliot called them, hers 'remind us of what nearly all children are'. She was 'without a rival' in the representation 'of what it is now fashionable to call "the lower middle class"' and had offered 'a new revelation of what society in quiet English parishes really is and has been'. She had 'given dignity to the life of boors and peasants in some of our bucolic districts, and this not by any concealment of their ignorance, follies, and frailties'.

But others balked. *Adam Bede* unflinchingly shows the desperation of Hetty who, having had sex with Arthur, waits for her period: after 'the on-coming of her great dread', she 'waited and waited, in the blind vague hope that something would happen to set her free from her terror'. One critic was appalled by such 'obstetric accuracy of detail'; another enjoined Eliot to 'copy the old masters of the art, who, if they gave us a baby, gave it us all at once'. And *The Mill on the Floss* was too bleak. 'She knowingly forces *dis*agreeable people on us'; her characters were 'prosaic, selfish, nasty'. Ruskin was dismayed at where the trajectory of Eliot's realism had taken her: 'There is not a single person in the book of the smallest importance to anybody in the world but themselves, or whose qualities deserved so much as a line of printer's type in their description'. *Silas Marner*'s characters were 'Mean, boorish, heavy-witted'.

'Common' referred to personality as well as social status. (After *Silas Marner*, her focus was increasingly the middle classes.)

She aimed, the narrator stresses in *Scenes of Clerical Life*, to stimulate interest in people who are 'palpably and unmistakably commonplace', to represent the 'experience of an ordinary fellow-mortal'. Eliot was writing in the age of statistics—the Belgian mathematician Adolphe Quetelet introduced the concept of the 'average man' in 1835—and in the century that invented the census. 'At least eighty out of a hundred of your adult male fellow-Britons returned in the last census, are neither extraordinarily silly, nor extraordinarily wicked, nor extraordinarily wise', she continued. Fiction, not numbers, could probe who they were. But how to represent ordinary people without being dull? How to bring out the intensity of ordinary lives without them ceasing to be ordinary? And how to bring out the individuality of characters who were familiar types?

One way—some might say a slightly awkward way—Eliot solves these difficulties is by repeatedly portraying unusual people in collision (a word she often uses) with ordinary people. After all, unusual people exist too. And so she 'will not pretend' of Adam 'that his was an ordinary character among workmen'; Maggie is 'unusual'; Silas is 'regarded as an exceptional person'; Eppie is 'not quite a common village maiden'; and both Romola and Dorothea are saintly. In contrast, Tom Tulliver, say, is 'one of those lads that grow everywhere in England'.

This solution wasn't without its difficulties. Nothing Eliot wrote ever produced more outrage than her decision to have the exceptional Maggie fall in love with the commonplace Stephen. She had tried to forestall criticism: Stephen's 'provincial, amateur' singing would not have impressed a 'well-educated young lady', but Maggie had just returned 'from a third-rate schoolroom', knows nothing of men, and is hungry for love. And striking women sometimes fall for bland men. Readers wanted none of it: the poet Swinburne read the third volume in a state of 'incredulous rage' and felt the urge to whip the 'cur'. Eliot's male characters have often been found wanting—Felix Holt is a 'grand *stump* of a character', Will Ladislaw 'a woman's man', Daniel Deronda the 'Prince of Prigs'—but the 'hairdresser's block' Stephen has attracted the greatest disgust.

Eliot's more daring move, best managed in her later novels, was to delve into the psychology of 'commonplace' people rather than make them the foil for more striking characters. In *Middlemarch*, what she memorably calls 'spots of commonness' are unavoidable. *Middlemarch* is about watching oneself fail to live up to the ideals of one's youth, shown through the trajectories of Lydgate (who will never become a great scientist), Casaubon (who will never become a great scholar), and Dorothea (who will never become a modern saint).

Her last novel *Daniel Deronda*, which strays furthest from the humble settings of her early fiction, maintains this focus on mediocrity. Eliot achieves in Gwendolen an exquisite portrait of a woman whose idea of herself as exceptional is offset by the narrow circle in which that exceptionality exerts any sway—by neighbours 'as middling as mid-day market'. Gwendolen fights an increasingly hopeless battle against the horrifying fate (to her) of being 'middling'. Her ambitions for a grandiose marriage that 'would not be of a middling kind' are revealed to be painfully misguided, as are those for fame as a singer, given her 'middling' voice. Daniel, meanwhile, is contentedly commonplace, taking 'any second-rateness in himself simply as a fact'. Eliot can be sarcastic, but she never sneers at them as a novelist like Thackeray might have done.

Commonplace events

The problem of reconciling plots with a realist faithfulness to ordinary events may have been even harder than that of drawing complex ordinary characters. Here, the Dutch paintings Eliot admired had the clear upper hand. So did poets: Eliot thought that a writer like William Cowper managed to invest the 'commonest objects', say 'the spoutless teapot holding a bit of mignionette that serves to cheer the dingy town-lodging', with lyric beauty and significance. But a novel?

Nineteenth-century novelists liked to fantasize—and sometimes joke—about plotless novels. Gustave Flaubert dreamed of writing 'a book about nothing', which 'would have almost no subject or at least in which the subject would be almost invisible, if such a thing is possible'. A character in George Gissing's *fin-de-siècle* novel *New Grub Street* imagines writing *Mr Bailey, Grocer*, a novel so doggedly realist that it would reproduce Bailey's life 'verbatim, without one single impertinent suggestion of any point of view save that of honest reporting. The result will be something unutterably tedious. Precisely. That is the stamp of the ignobly decent life. If it were anything *but* tedious it would be untrue.'

Eliot didn't want to 'invent thrilling incidents' for her readers' 'amusement' when most people experience 'no hairbreadth escapes or thrilling adventures'. 'Tragedy' shouldn't depend on 'ermine tippets, adultery, and murder', *Scenes of Clerical Life* contended. Easier said than done. Hetty Sorrel has premarital sex, is put on trial for murder, and is rescued from the scaffold in a hairbreadth escape. There is adultery and murder in *Romola*, adultery and manslaughter in *Felix Holt*. We are even treated to a sable tippet, courtesy of aunt Glegg in *The Mill on the Floss*.

Just as remarkable people exist among those who are 'far from remarkable', it could be claimed that ordinary lives sometimes are punctuated by extraordinary events. Certainly, Eliot could point to the fact that *Adam Bede* was based on the experience of her Methodist aunt Samuel, who in 1802 had visited Mary Voce before she was executed for murdering her child. But it also became a disingenuous tactic amongst the more sensational Victorian novelists to claim that their outlandish plots had some basis in fact. Dickens even used this ploy to justify Krook's spontaneous combustion in *Bleak House*. Anything might be proved on the back of a newspaper anecdote, but it was hardly in the spirit of Eliot's realist doctrine to do so.

Felix Holt reads like a failed experiment in squaring this circle. There are French lovers—Annette and Maurice—who each possess half a locket. The queen-like demeanour of a lower-middle-class girl strikes everyone until it's revealed that she is, indeed, the heir to a fortune, a revelation that works no better here than it does in *Oliver Twist*. An illegitimate child horsewhips the man who reveals, in italics, '*I am your father*'. Insistent references to literary conventions—'You are quite in another *genre*', Esther tells Harold, who can't believe she'll 'make a ballad heroine of herself' by marrying the working-class Felix—suggest that Eliot is deliberately exploring the idea that romance can still befall unremarkable people in an unremarkable town. But the line between this and actual melodrama is too fine, and the result is unconvincing.

Felix Holt fails because ordinary melodrama feels like an irresolvable contradiction: melodrama is predicated on the idea of exaggeration. She was far more successful in showing that tragedy could exist in ordinary life, above all in *The Mill on the Floss*. There, she draws on two models of classical tragedy. The first is that of a man brought down by his fatal flaw. Although Mr Tulliver is 'nothing more than a superior miller', his 'Hotspur temperament' gives his trajectory affinities with that 'far-echoing tragedy, which sweeps the stage in regal robes'. The second is that, more congenial to Eliot, of the clash between equally defensible yet incompatible claims, embodied by Maggie straining to reconcile her natural promptings with familial obligations.

Eliot admired Sophocles' *Antigone*, whose protagonist is torn between a desire to stay true to her brother and the duty she owes the state and her father. She wrote an article extolling how the play presents the 'dramatic collision' of 'two principles, both having their validity'. King Creon is no tyrant and Antigone is not blameless: each 'is contending for what he believes to be the right'. Eliot had framed *The Mill on the Floss* in a similar fashion for Blackwood: 'the exhibition of the *right* on both sides being the very soul of my intention in the story' (III.397). The narrator comments of Maggie that, 'when there is this contrast between the outward and the inward', 'painful collisions come of it'. The predicted collision becomes all too literal at the novel's conclusion, when she drowns after being hit by a large piece of machinery.

Many have also found this ending dissatisfying because it betrays the intuition expressed elsewhere in the novel that the real tragedy of most lives takes the form of endurance rather than events. Eliot suggested this, with increasing deftness, throughout her career. Having spent years repressing her ambitions to look after her father, she knew what it was like to feel *'walled-in'* (I.71). She often writes about how monotony makes difficult situations harder: waiting rather than acting, repeating identical tasks with no expectation of relief. 'There is something sustaining in the very agitation that accompanies the first shocks of trouble', she writes in *The Mill on the Floss*. Despair comes afterwards, 'when sorrow has become stale, and has no longer an emotive intensity that counteracts its pain', when 'day follows day in dull unexpectant sameness, and trial is a dreary routine'.

In 1866 the *Times* journalist E. S. Dallas took stock of the 'feminine influence' he believed was taking over fiction. He was troubled: 'this feminine tendency in our literature is not all for good'. The problem wasn't one of propriety, but of plot. Novels, he wrote, were about action, but 'when women are the chief characters, how are you to set them in motion? The life of women cannot well be described as a life of action.' Putting women at the heart of a novel meant putting them 'into a false position', tempting novelists into excesses (such as having women commit

crimes) or vulgarity (having them undertake 'masculine deeds').
Realist female protagonists, evidently, were an oxymoron.

Instead, Eliot redefined what a realist protagonist might do, in
part by making monotony itself the subject. She is entirely
convincing when she portrays Maggie's envy of Tom, who can
react to the family bankruptcy by taking a job, or Gwendolen's
anxious, puzzled sense that her mother's quiet dreariness is not
due to some incident in her past, but is 'the ordinary result of
women's experience'. This was a human truth, and not just a
feminine one. 'What duty is made of a single difficult resolve?', she
asks in *Daniel Deronda*, adding that the 'difficulty lies in the daily
unflinching support of consequences that mar the blessed return
of morning with the prospect of irritation to be suppressed or
shame to be endured'.

Novels privilege single momentous events; reality consists of
repetition. Just as she developed an ability to represent people's
'spots of commonness', so did she find a way to adapt tragedy. In
her hands, the genre becomes capacious enough to respond to the
full range of human experience, and she found a new assuredness
in attending to the ordinary bewilderment of melancholy or
disappointment. Dorothea Brooke's heartache during her
honeymoon in Rome will probably not 'be regarded as tragic' by
readers, the narrator expects, for it 'is not unusual, and we do not
expect people to be deeply moved by what is not unusual'. Eliot no
longer needed to make her case defensively: the heartache is
deeply moving.

So is the commonplace disintegration of the Lydgates' marriage.
Henry James perfectly conveys the 'pathos' of these scenes,
which are

> deepened by the constantly low key in which they are pitched. It is a
> tragedy based on unpaid butchers' bills, and the urgent need for small
> economies. The author has desired to be strictly real and to adhere to

the facts of the common lot, and she has given us a powerful version of that typical human drama, the struggles of an ambitious soul with sordid disappointments and vulgar embarrassments.

The limits of realism

Eliot became increasingly audacious in the way she confronted head-on the fact that art wasn't—indeed never could be, and shouldn't aspire to be—like life. *Middlemarch* and *Daniel Deronda* preserve her allegiance to the ordinary even as they draw attention to the artificiality of the medium that aspires to encompass it. One of the most famous passages in all of Eliot's novels comes as the reader is sucked into the 'dreary oppression' of Dorothea's withering marriage to Casaubon. Chapter 29 opens:

> One morning some weeks after her arrival at Lowick, Dorothea—but why always Dorothea? Was her point of view the only possible one with regard to this marriage? I protest against all our interest, all our effort at understanding being given to the young skins that look blooming in spite of trouble; for these too will get faded, and will know the older and more eating griefs which we are helping to neglect. In spite of the blinking eyes and white moles objectionable to Celia, and the want of muscular curve which was morally painful to Sir James, Mr Casaubon had an intense consciousness within him, and was spiritually a-hungered like the rest of us.

This extraordinary Copernican shift meets the perspectival challenge that, like Dorothea, 'Mr Casaubon, too, was the centre of his own world'. It's about the bias of novelists and the narrow pool of types from which they choose protagonists. It's about the bias of readers who would rather hear about those types. It's about the human inevitability of believing ourselves the hero of our own drama. It's about the difficult duty of recognizing that even those people by whom we feel instinctively put off are, as

Mary Garth had earlier shrugged, interesting to themselves. Exhibiting Eliot's lifelong concern with self-checking, the interruption addresses the inevitable selections and exclusions all artists are forced to make. To quote the passage as an independent clause as writers sometimes do ('But why always Dorothea?') is to miss, quite literally, its stroke of genius.

Eliot had always kept the reader alive to the rich lives of her minor characters, making us feel that they too hold novels waiting to be written. We feel this in *Adam Bede* with Bartle Massey, whose hints that he was once in trouble are never elaborated, or in *The Mill on the Floss* when the gentle revelation that Tom loves Lucy Deane lets us glimpse at what the novel might have looked like from the perspective of his own frustrations and sacrifices. This famous interruption, though, is her most explicit recognition of a problem about form. Further self-checking is required to curtail the instinct to include ever-more perspectives in *Middlemarch*. The narrator nearly falls into another narrative strand, this one about the minor character Joshua Rigg, before pulling back: 'Enough. We are concerned with looking at Joshua Rigg's sale of his land from Mr Bulstrode's point of view.'

Daniel Deronda appears, in many ways, like the result of Eliot's experiments in *Middlemarch*. Where does the novel even begin? The habit Eliot developed from *Romola* of including chapter epigraphs, some by other writers and some of her own devising, means the novel starts twice, once with the epigraph and once with the narrative. But here the question of beginnings is the very subject of the epigraph, which opens, 'Men can do nothing without the make-believe of a beginning'. Where novels start and stop are also the result of inclusions and exclusions and, Eliot makes us feel, of chance. Appropriately for a novel about gambling, the novel might start here or land elsewhere. E. M. Forster began his 1910 novel *Howards End* with a similar gesture: 'One may as well begin with Helen's letters to her sister'.

Both acknowledge the arbitrariness of fictional starting points, but whereas Forster sounds weary of, or perhaps careless about, the need to go through novelistic motions, Eliot is making a more precise point about perspective and how we make meaning.

She doubles down, starting the narrative proper with a question: 'Was she beautiful or not beautiful?' As if '—but why always Dorothea?' had set something off, *Daniel Deronda* bursts with an unprecedented number of questions. Everything here is up for debate: characters don't know each other (Daniel is 'enigmatic to his friends'), don't know themselves ('was it triumph she felt most or terror?'), and free indirect discourse can make the characters seem opaque to the narrator ('Where was the good of choice coming again? What did she wish? Anything different?'). The ending leaves the question of whether Gwendolen contributed to Grandcourt's death unresolved and Daniel's trajectory unclear. The interjections typical of Eliot's narrators are here often put as questions ('What should we all do without the calendar, when we want to put off a disagreeable duty?'). She even expresses impatience at her impossible task: 'Attempts at description are stupid: who can all at once describe a human being?'

No one can, and so the novel starts in the middle. The first scene shows Gwendolen's and Daniel's first meeting before slowly retracing the steps leading up to it. First-person novels like Emily Brontë's *Wuthering Heights* often play with chronology, but starting in the middle is more unusual for a Victorian novel with an omniscient narrator. Like science, the epigraph notes, 'Poetry has always been understood to start in the middle', but not novels. The experiment, first attempted in 'Mr Gilfil's Love-Story', is part of Eliot's conviction that people, fictional or real, can only be understood over time, in context, and from multiple angles. As she writes in another epigraph, 'the narrator of human actions' would ideally be able to 'thread the hidden pathways of feeling and thought which lead up to every moment of action'. We see

Gwendolen's boldness and Daniel's sympathetic concern around the gambling table twice, first while they are entirely mysterious to us and then when they are not. Eliot wants us to notice the evolution in our responses: above all, she wants us to notice how understanding them better has acted on our sympathies.

Chapter 3
Sympathy

Was George Eliot 'the first great *godless* writer of fiction that has appeared in England', as the Catholic novelist W. H. Mallock declared in 1879? The word agnostic, which first appeared in the late 1860s, may suit her better than atheist. She fought her own 'Holy War', but later reproached a friend for thinking she could ever wish to 'rob a man of his religious belief' (IV.64). Her first book, published in 1846, was a translation of David Strauss's *The Life of Jesus, Critically Examined*, a work of German biblical scholarship that fed the century's growing religious scepticism by sifting the myths about Jesus from historical facts. But as she translated, she kept pictures of Jesus on her desk and recoiled from the way Strauss stripped Christianity of its poetry. Such behaviour looks conflicted, but in fact expressed her brand of humanism.

The 19th-century French philosopher Auguste Comte attempted to establish an international 'religion of humanity'. As someone with a lifelong wariness of systematic thinking, Eliot was never likely to become a fully paid-up member of his scheme to create a new secular calendar worshipping Great Men from Moses to Bichat. The calendar was the slightly ludicrous extension of a philosophy that did, however, pique her interest: positivism. A founder of sociology (he coined the word in 1838), Comte explained the development of religion anthropologically.

Faith moved through three stages: theological (during which men believe in personified gods, or a God, and interpret the world through supernatural phenomena), metaphysical (during which God becomes abstract), and finally Positivist (when the world is analysed empirically). The trajectory could apply to both societies and individuals. The main idea Eliot took from Comte is that there is no abrupt rupture between religious faith in God and secular faith in humankind. Rather, the first prepares the ground for the second. When Maggie is attached to her wooden 'Fetish' (a doll), or when Silas clings to his earthenware pot, these are manifestations of a Comtean 'primitive' fetishism preparing them for wider human attachments.

A second philosopher, the German Ludwig Feuerbach, had a more profound influence on Eliot: 'With the ideas of Feuerbach I everywhere agree' (II.153). Her 1854 translation of his book *The Essence of Christianity* is the only work that ever appeared under her own name, Marian Evans. Like Comte, Feuerbach interpreted religion anthropologically, but the result is warmer. Feuerbach's core idea is that God is a projection of man's beliefs about man or, as he put it (in Eliot's translation): 'the divine being is nothing else than the human being'. He articulates a humanist conviction of man's capacity for good since, Eliot clarified for a fellow agnostic, 'the idea of God' is in fact 'the ideal of a goodness entirely human' (VI.98).

His philosophy is one of interdependence. Feuerbach emphasized the relationship between self and other and the ways in which the other becomes part of the self:

> Man is himself at once I and thou; he can put himself in the place of another, for this reason, that to him his species, his essential nature, and not merely his individuality, is an object of thought.

Eliot's novels enact Feuerbach's statement that 'The relations of child and parent, of husband and wife, of brother and friend—in general, of man to man—in short, all the moral relations are *per se* religious'. We see it, for instance, when the narrator lingers on Seth Bede's feelings for Dinah: 'Love of this sort is hardly distinguishable from religious feeling'. *The Times* astutely summarized the novel as a 'secular rendering of the deepest sentiment of Christianity'.

Eliot gained from Feuerbach further confirmation of her position that people didn't need dogmas and religious institutions. These often kept individuals apart, became lost in metaphysics rather than serving human needs, and at their worst preached judgement instead of kindness. The 'inspiring principle which alone gives me courage to write', she explained, was that of giving readers:

> a clearer conception and a more active admiration of those vital elements which bind men together and give a higher worthiness to their existence; and also to help them in gradually dissociating these elements from the more transient forms on which an outworn teaching tends to make them dependent. (IV.472)

So carefully does Eliot introduce the idea of religion as a temporary stepping-stone that it was not until after her death, when Cross's biography revealed her early loss of her faith, that many realized they'd been enjoying humanist fiction all along. As we saw above, before the mystery of Eliot's pseudonym was solved, speculations were rife that *Scenes of Clerical Life* and *Adam Bede* were written by a clergyman. A devout reader copied excerpts from *Romola* into her bible. She was even consulted for religious advice.

Not 'godless', then, but poised between two worlds. The position—some might say compromise—Eliot reached has been read very differently. The iconoclastic philosopher Nietzsche was scornful that, having 'got rid of the Christian god', Eliot, like many of her contemporaries, felt 'obliged to cling all the more firmly to Christian morality'. The early 20th-century historian G. M. Young, on the contrary, felt inclined to side with those who felt Eliot 'saved us from the moral catastrophe which might have been expected to follow upon the waning of religious conviction'.

Eliot didn't subscribe to the notion of art for art's sake: she meant for her novels to do good. She hoped her readers would 'be better able to *imagine* and to *feel* the pains and the joys of those who differ from themselves in everything but the broad fact of being struggling erring human creatures' (III.111). Crucially, she believed that

> æsthetic teaching is the highest of all teaching because it deals with life in its highest complexity. But if it ceases to be purely æsthetic—if it lapses anywhere from the picture to the diagram—it becomes the most offensive of all teaching. (IV.300)

To make the very form of the novels act on us so that we can then feel more for the beings outside them was the formidable task she set herself.

Omniscient narrators

When a reader claims they do not like George Eliot, what they often mean is that they don't like her narrators. Eliot wrote that she 'always exercised a severe watch against anything that could be called preaching' (V.459), but the question of whether she succeeded has often come down to how she handles narrative voice. Her narrators aren't just omniscient: they're omnipresent. As one reviewer summarized: 'At every turn reflections are introduced upon the characters, upon the events, upon the way the characters and the events work upon one another.' For his part, he admired the running commentary—its thoughts were original, its moral reflections subtle—but he couldn't deny that it might annoy others. It clearly annoyed an American critic, who found her novels 'too much like treatises on human nature, anecdotically illustrated'.

Her early narrators certainly aren't shy in drawing attention to the teaching taking place, or at least being attempted. For instance, in *Scenes of Clerical Life*:

> Depend upon it, you would gain unspeakably if you would learn with me to see some of the poetry and the pathos, the tragedy and the comedy, lying in the experience of a human soul that looks out through dull grey eyes, and that speaks in a voice of quite ordinary tones.

Or here, in *The Mill on the Floss*:

> I share with you this sense of oppressive narrowness; but it is necessary that we should feel it, if we care to understand how it acted on the lives of Tom and Maggie.

An Edwardian working-class memoirist recalled having read Eliot's novels as a precocious 9-year-old, but 'solely for the story. I used to skip the parts that moralized, or painted verbal scenery, a practice at which I became very dexterous.' Ought it to be so obvious to see which parts might be skipped?

Successful orators in Eliot's novels show none of what she describes in *Scenes of Clerical Life* as 'the self-satisfied unction of the teacher, quoting, or exhorting, or expounding'. The case for the prosecution might point to those instances when her readers are exhorted to overcome a resistance which in all likelihood they don't feel. 'If you blame Mr Riley very severely for giving a recommendation on such slight grounds, I must say you are rather hard upon him', she scolds in *The Mill on the Floss*; 'Pray think no ill of Miss Noble', we are urged in *Middlemarch*. (Has anyone ever thought ill of Miss Noble?) These pleas are made with a smile, but one reviewer expostulated that 'our authoress keeps groaning out her tiresome tirades against evils for the most part of her own imagining'. Eliot sceptics see such comments as the irritating intrusions of an author willing to interrupt her story to get something off her chest which she would have done better saving for a preface or after-dinner chat (Figure 5).

5. Readers often conflated George Eliot—pictured here in 1858—with her wise narrators and swamped her with advice letters.

They overlook how the narrators embody her ideas rather than merely acting as overbearing authorial mouthpieces. They are what we might call personalized omniscient narrators: they have access to the thoughts of all the characters, but speak in the first person, sometimes prefacing their thoughts with 'for my part', 'it seems to me', or 'I have often wondered'. In her early fiction, Eliot flirted with the concept of a homodiegetic narrator, that is to say a narrator who also participates in the story, but she stopped short: hers don't affect the plot and are barely characterized.

In *Scenes of Clerical Life*, *Adam Bede*, and *The Mill on the Floss*, the narrators are male. He remembers having been kept quiet with bread-and-butter as a baby in Shepperton Church and misbehaving in the pews. He once had a chat with *Adam Bede*. He begins *The Mill on the Floss* in a doze, collects local history manuscripts, and knows what it's like to play billiards. In *Felix Holt*, the narrator gently mocks Mr Lyon's harmless pretentious acts, before adding:

> I confess to smiling myself, being sceptical as to the effect of ardent appeals and nice distinctions on gentlemen who are got up, both inside and out, as candidates in the style of the period; but I never smiled at Mr Lyon's trustful energy without falling to penitence and veneration immediately after.

The slip from omniscient narrator to character is almost imperceptible.

These are blink-and-you-miss-it moments, occurring less than a handful of times in each novel and sometimes only once. Every time, we're being asked to accept a logical impossibility: the narrators can't both be neighbours and have access to other characters' private thoughts. So why does Eliot do it? It's a narrative counterpart to her conception of religious humanism: an omniscient narration adapted to a secular world in which faith in godlike perspectives has been shaken. It puts the narrator among rather than above the characters, stressing connection rather than detachment. As she writes of a character in *Scenes of Clerical Life*, 'I am not poised at that lofty height. I am on the level and in the press with him.' And it's profoundly human. She had once explained to Blackwood: 'I only try to exhibit some things as they have been or are, seen through such a medium as my own nature gives me' (II.362). This didn't mean that she could only write about herself—far from it—but she recognized that no perspective could avoid the impress of subjectivity.

Eliot's only experiment with first-person narration, 'The Lifted Veil', is revealing. In some ways, the short story sneaks in omniscience through the back door by telling the story of a man who can hear other people's thoughts. But here the narrator clamours for our compassion directly: 'Are you unable to give me your sympathy—you who read this?' Latimer is the type of plaintive figure Eliot succeeds in making us care for elsewhere, but when such a man is the sole narrator the effect is off-putting. Imagine *The Mill on the Floss* narrated entirely by Stephen Guest. Eliot admired in Goethe, one of her favourite writers, his 'large tolerance' for a 'mixed and erring' humanity. Eliot's omniscient narrators, themselves mixed and erring, are likewise there to encourage generosity.

The power of comparison

There was something, Eliot believed, that could strengthen sympathy: 'I will ask you to use your power of comparison a little more effectively', she requests in *Middlemarch*. The analogies that are a hallmark of her style model this power for us. '[I]t is a narrow mind which cannot look at a subject from various points of view', she warns in the same novel, adding later that the mind is made 'flexible with constant comparison'. 'But beware of arriving at conclusions without comparison', we're reminded in *Daniel Deronda*.

Eliot began writing fiction a few weeks after a holiday spent scampering around the Devon coast trawling for specimens Lewes could use in his physiological research. The journal she kept shows how scientific observation aligned with her ideas about fiction. She was struck, for example, by old houses that looked like mollusc shells and began to think of the likeness between humans and other species that appropriate houses for themselves. Back in London, the day after she began her first story, Eliot and Lewes bought their first microscope.

Scientific observations often buttress her explanations of how we might come to a better understanding of ordinary lives. Regarding the Tullivers:

> we need not shrink from this comparison of small things with great; for does not science tell us that its highest striving is after the ascertainment of a unity which shall bind the smallest things with the greatest?

In *Middlemarch*, 'Even with a microscope directed on a water-drop we find ourselves making interpretations which turn out to be rather coarse', depending on whether we use a weak or a stronger lens, an appropriate image for a novel preoccupied with scientific discovery and subtitled 'A Study of Provincial Life'. The doctor Lydgate supplies other comparisons, echoing the narrator in his own claim that '"a man's mind must be continually expanding and shrinking between the whole human horizon and the horizon of an object-glass"'. Eliot sees her novels working in a similar way as a process of expansion and contraction between the panorama and the nearly imperceptible movements of a single mind.

She thought of this in terms of optical instruments but also human biology. One of her favourite images was that of the heart. Lydgate is adamant that '"there must be a systole and diastole in all inquiry"'. The diastole is when the heart dilates, its chambers filling with blood; the systole is when it contracts and expels blood into the arteries. Feuerbach used it metaphorically too. Life 'consists in a perpetual systole and diastole', as did faith: 'In the religious systole man propels his own nature for himself, he throws himself outward; in the religious diastole he receives the rejected nature into his heart again.' Eliot understood sympathy to work through a similar process—the self was thrown outward towards another and brought back into the self—but also novels. Omniscient narration was an essential tool for her because, in being able to range between perspectives, it can do what people can't, just as we rely on a lens to see the creatures swirling inside a water-drop.

The fluid movement between self and other takes place at the smaller level of syntax too, here in *The Mill on the Floss*:

> And as we are all apt to believe what the world believes about us, it was his habit to think of failure and ruin with the same sort of remote pity with which a spare, long-necked man hears that his plethoric short-necked neighbour is stricken with apoplexy.

This single sentence shifts from a very human 'we', putting the narrator and reader side by side, as a step towards a comparison with Mr Tulliver's perspective, before stretching out to another comparison, this time embracing a more abstract, fable-like vision. As so often with Eliot, they're comparisons about the act of comparing. The constant reminder of perspectives is meant to teach, not through contained, portable morality, but through movement.

Fellow-feeling

What Eliot sought to teach is summarized in *Middlemarch:* 'There is no general doctrine which is not capable of eating out our morality if unchecked by the deep-seated habit of direct fellow-feeling with individual fellow-men.' Eliot kept coming back to the word 'fellow-feeling'. As she set out in *Adam Bede*, fiction should stimulate emotions that we then use to extend our sympathy with the 'real breathing men and women' who 'can be cheered and helped onward by your fellow-feeling, your forbearance, your outspoken, brave justice'.

Fellow-feeling relied on that consciousness of human 'interdependence' (she uses the word in *Middlemarch*) which novels were uniquely able to give. Interdependence is, in some ways, the flipside of the 'hampering' narrowness of provincial life. The critic Gillian Beer rightly observes that 'George Eliot's interest is in relationships. "Independence" did not stir her artistically.' This is all the more striking given that Eliot was writing in the great age of self-help (Samuel Smiles's work of that name became a best-seller the same year as *Adam Bede*) and Emersonian self-reliance. Eliot admired Thoreau's nature writing, but she would have found the man who chose to leave Walden's woods more compelling than the one who entered them.

She joined countless 19th-century philosophers, scientists, and novelists in using the image of the web. '"The prosperity of the country is one web"', exclaims a retired hosier during a pub debate in *Felix Holt*. The image is flexible, used in *Middlemarch* to describe plot ('all the light I can command must be concentrated on this particular web'), love (Rosamond and Lydgate 'spinning industriously at the mutual web'), and science (the body consists 'of certain primary webs or tissues'). Across the novels, characters are often linked by, and become entangled in, threads.

Relations between family members illustrate on a smaller scale the ties that connect us. In *Adam Bede*, Eliot describes how we bristle against our parents even as (or because) we come to resemble them:

> Nature, that great tragic dramatist, knits us together by bone and muscle, and divides us by the subtler web of our brains; blends yearning and repulsion; and ties us by our heartstrings to the beings that jar us at every movement.

The sentence conjures up the spinning Fates of classical mythology, here interwoven with human biology and psychology, as the sentence performs grammatically the kinds of connections it's describing: the links provided by commas and semicolons keep each clause separate yet combine them in one sentence. 'Blending' is an important word for Eliot and points to those processes by which the separate forces of self and other might harmonize.

Silas Marner is her exploration of how such harmonizing might work on a communal rather than domestic scale: it tells how Silas's 'history became blent in a singular manner with the life of his neighbours'. The ending of *The Mill on the Floss*—a character's scandalous expulsion from an unforgiving community—here becomes the starting point. The novella tracks how, driven to a condition of self-sufficiency, Silas is rescued 'from the insect-like existence into which his nature had shrunk', first by recognizing that 'if any help came to him it must come from without', and then through Eppie, who created 'fresh links between his life and the lives from which he had hitherto shrunk continually into narrower isolation'.

Interdependence means that our actions reverberate. As Irwine warns Adam Bede, '"Men's lives are as thoroughly blended with each other as the air they breathe."' *Daniel Deronda* is her most developed demonstration of what she called in an essay the 'inexorable law of consequences', as Gwendolen is brought to a full realization of the ripple effect of her decision to marry Grandcourt. The novel echoes with Daniel's warning that '"our gain is another's loss"'. Terrified of what she has done, Gwendolen seeks advice from Daniel, who urges:

> 'Turn your fear into a safeguard. Keep your dread fixed on the idea of increasing that remorse which is so bitter to you.... It is like quickness of hearing. It may make consequences passionately present to you. Try to take hold of your sensibility, and use it as if it were a faculty, like vision.'

His warning again recalls Feuerbach: 'My fellow-man is my objective conscience; he makes my failings a reproach to me; even when he does not expressly mention them, he is my personified feeling of shame.'

The task Eliot set herself of 'extending our contact with our fellow-men beyond the bounds of our personal lot' involves the form of her fiction as well as its contents. *The Mill on the Floss* is the only one of Eliot's novels that stays close to a single perspective. (We follow Tom to school, but he is eclipsed in adulthood.) All the others show the gradual convergence of two, three, four, or more characters. The narrator elaborates on this in *Middlemarch*:

> But any one watching keenly the stealthy convergence of human lots, sees a slow preparation of effects from one life on another, which tells like a calculated irony on the indifference or the frozen stare with which we look at our unintroduced neighbour. Destiny stands by sarcastic with our *dramatis personæ* folded in her hand.

'Blending' is a good word to describe how *Middlemarch* came to be. On 1 January 1869, Eliot recorded in her diary her objective to write 'A Novel called Middlemarch'—she'd been brooding on it since 1867, but other projects got in the way. She began writing about Lydgate, then stalled, incapacitated by self-doubt. A year after laying the manuscript down, she began a different story called 'Miss Brooke', begun 'without any very serious intention of carrying it out lengthily'. Later, over lunch with Blackwood, she announced she'd combine the two. The 'stealthy convergence of human lots' is as much a description of human interdependence as it is of the novel's genesis, which also helps to account for the unprecedentedly large cast of characters whose perspective Eliot takes the time to give.

Not all of Eliot's readers have been willing to accept the demands she places on them. One reviewer didn't like having his attention divided in this fashion and suggested it wouldn't take much to publish separately the Dorothea–Casaubon plot, the Lydgate–Rosamond plot, and the Fred–Mary plot. (He would have felt vindicated had he known the novel's origin story.) His proposal anticipates that of the mid-20th-century critic F. R. Leavis, who found the Gwendolen plot of *Daniel Deronda* one of Eliot's greatest achievements and the Daniel plot one of her most tedious, and began rescuing the novel by preparing an edition (later abandoned) consisting entirely of Gwendolen's story.

Both responses would have horrified Eliot, who would have seen in them a failure of art and sympathy. In an 1868 essay called 'Notes on Form in Art', published posthumously, she speculated that the 'highest example of Form' is 'the relation of multiplex interdependent parts to a whole which is itself in the most varied & therefore the fullest relation to other wholes'. She lends the visionary Mordecai in *Daniel Deronda* similar thoughts: 'Now, in complete unity a part possesses the whole as the whole possesses every part.' Although she struggled with publishing her novels in instalments, doing so would have sharpened this vision of form.

Middlemarch's first readers lived with it for 13 months: it appeared between December 1871 and December 1872. One reviewer felt this contributed to the novel's powerful effect: 'those will understand it best and value it most who have made acquaintance slowly during the past year with all its characters, and discussed them eagerly with their friends, in all the various stages of their growth and fortune'. A reader stopped Eliot on London's Regent Street to share her anxiety about Lydgate. A visitor remembered Lewes 'holding me by the button as he announced to me in confidence . . . , "Celia is going to have a baby!"'

From her earliest works, Eliot drew attention to the process whereby readers grow into sympathy. 'See the difference between the impression a man makes on you when you walk by his side in

59

familiar talk, or look at him in his home, and the figure he makes when seen from a lofty historical level', she writes in *Adam Bede*. She encourages us to see how we've gradually tuned into the frequency of each character, with comments like: 'His work, as you know, had always been part of his religion' (of Adam Bede), and 'From what you know of her, you will not be surprised that she threw exaggeration and wilfulness, some pride and impetuosity, even into her self-renunciation' (of Maggie). Eliot doesn't ask us to identify with her characters, but to respond to them as familiars.

The limits of sympathy

Feuerbach wrote that it was not 'until man has reached an advanced stage of culture that he can double himself, so as to play the part of another within himself'. Writing in a Darwinian age, Eliot knew that evolution did not happen overnight. It's easy to feel for a fictional character; it's harder to feel for a person. Her characters don't have the benefit of an omniscient narrator who can shine a light on the thoughts and needs of the people around them; they struggle alone.

Eliot depicts characters with little notion of any interiority beyond themselves (such as Hetty, Tessa, Rosamond, and initially Gwendolen), and those with an almost supra-human capacity for sympathy (including Dinah, Romola, Dorothea, and Daniel). She enjoyed representing climactic scenes in which they come together: Dinah visits Hetty in prison, Romola comes to Tessa's aid, Dorothea seeks out a miserable Rosamond, Daniel supports Gwendolen. The sympathetic natures don't effect anything like a transformation of the narrower ones—that would be too facile—but offer them a glimpse of the strength that comes from fellow-feeling. Other characters fall somewhere in the middle. For many, sympathy is acquired, often learnt through pain or sorrow which Eliot frequently describes as a baptism. Sympathy is not instinctive but takes resolve, like that of Nancy who, faced with

Godfrey's confession that he has a daughter he never claimed, is shown 'trying, with pre-determined sympathy, to see everything as Godfrey saw it'.

The novels illustrate a range of sympathetic emotions. Pity is the least taxing. Narrators and characters find it equally effortless to offer it: 'Poor child!', 'Poor Dorothea!', 'Poor Mary', 'poor father', and so on. Pity requires minimal imaginative engagement—it's a sympathetic warm-up. Exercising the muscle of sympathy already entails a harder endeavour to find common ground. For Feuerbach, 'I feel only . . . for that in which I feel myself, whose sufferings I myself suffer. Sympathy presupposes a like nature.' Or, as Eliot puts it in *Scenes of Clerical Life*, 'sympathy is but a living again through our own past in a new form'. Philip Wakem's sensitivity about his disability, for example, is what makes him feel for Tom Tulliver when he injures his foot. We're invited to use our 'power of comparison' in a similar way: to better understand Adam Bede's infatuation for Hetty, the reader is asked whether they were ever over-indulgent towards a pretty woman.

But fellow-feeling would be a blunt tool if it depended on pre-existing sympathetic bonds. Conveying Hetty's charm to someone who has never been struck by a beautiful woman is as pointless as painting the 'charms of a bright spring day' if 'you had never in your life utterly forgotten yourself in straining your eyes after the mounting lark'. And so we are asked to undertake the hardest exercise of all: sympathy for those who feel perplexingly alien to us. There is no straightforward pulling of the heart-strings here: the path of sympathy, like realism, is unglamorous. The 'abandonment of egoism', Eliot writes in *The Mill on the Floss*, involves the 'steep highway of tolerance, just allowance, and self-blame, where there are no leafy honours to be gathered and worn'. It's hard for Eliot too: 'The last refuge of intolerance is in not tolerating the intolerant—and I am often in danger of secreting that sort of venom' (II.402), she admitted to a friend.

Still. Neither the novel nor fellow-feeling can be limitless if it is to exist in any meaningful way. She considers this in global terms. It is legitimate, she maintained in an essay called 'The Modern Hep! Hep! Hep!', to feel more for those closest to us; 'Affection, intelligence, duty, radiate from a centre, and nature has decided that for us English folk that centre' is England. The key—and a vital argument against imperialist conquest—is to remember that other nations feel equally strongly about their own centre: 'we should recognise a corresponding attachment to nationality as legitimate in every other people'.

In the fiction, the necessary boundaries of sympathy are expressed in a more individual manner. We witness Daniel Deronda attempting a kind of Stoic exercise:

> He was forgetting everything else in a half-speculative, half-involuntary identification of himself with the objects he was looking at, thinking how far it might be possible habitually to shift his centre till his own personality would be no less outside him than the landscape,—when the sense of something moving on the bank opposite him where it was bordered by a line of willow bushes, made him turn his glance thitherward.

As so often in Eliot, interruption carries out an important check, here in the form of real life calling Daniel away from abstraction. The point is that it appears like a thought experiment, something theoretic rather than practical, sustainable, or even desirable.

Eliot's most famous acknowledgement of sympathy's necessary boundaries again takes place in *Middlemarch*. Will Ladislaw warns that the exclusive devotion to others that makes Dorothea unable to enjoy anything which other people can't share is a '"fanaticism of sympathy"'. Will has vested interests—he wants Dorothea to enjoy *him*—but the narrator shares his concerns. During her honeymoon in Rome, Dorothea is in low spirits, which Eliot considers a common enough emotion for young brides. Then adds:

> That element of tragedy which lies in the very fact of frequency, has not yet wrought itself into the coarse emotion of mankind; and perhaps our frames could hardly bear much of it. If we had a keen vision and feeling of all ordinary human life, it would be like hearing the grass grow and the squirrel's heart beat, and we should die of that roar which lies on the other side of silence. As it is, the quickest of us walk about well wadded with stupidity.

'Frequency' means repetition, but the word reverberates with another meaning: from the 1830s it was used in physics to describe the recurrence of sound, here set off by association. Evolution haunts the passage, with the word 'yet' invoking the possibility of development in our physiology as in technology— after all, we *can* now hear the squirrel's heartbeat and have survived to tell the tale. But science and emotion remain tantalizingly apart. The 'fact' of pain contrasts with the speculative nature of sympathy ('perhaps', 'if', 'it would be like') mimicking the gap between life and art that Dorothea can't imagine closing. The passage probes what both people and art can't do, yet what it doesn't account for is the effect of its own cadences and movement between contraction, expansion, and contraction. It is almost impossible to read without vibrating too.

Chapter 4
Cognition

'"You see, it was really George Eliot who started it all…It was she who started putting all the action inside."' Identifying literary 'firsts' is a risky venture, but it would be hard to better D. H. Lawrence's candidate for the originator of English psychological fiction. Eliot herself described her writing as 'simply a set of experiments in life—an endeavour to see what our thought and emotion may be capable of' (VI.216). As a character in *Daniel Deronda* proposes, '"thoughts, feelings, apparitions in the darkness are events—are they not?"' Eliot believed they were.

Her conviction was of a piece with the realist determination to bring to light the everyday experiences overlooked by novelists and misunderstood by readers: it was to examine what Samuel Taylor Coleridge called 'the *drama* of Reason', that which could 'present the thought growing'. As she asserts in *Adam Bede*, 'Our mental business is carried on much in the same way as the business of the State: a great deal of hard work is done by agents who are not acknowledged.' Fittingly, Freud thought that her novels—*Middlemarch* in particular—helped 'illuminate' his own relationships.

George Meredith wrote a novel called *The Egoist*, but surely no 19th-century writer gave more sustained attention to the psychology of egoism than Eliot. There are those characters in whom egoism has the decided upper hand: the parasitic Countess Czerlaski in 'Amos Barton'; 'pigeon-like' Hetty Sorrel, strutting about her room as she daydreams an impossible future with the self-justifying Arthur Donnithorne; the irresponsible, blackmailing Dunstan Cass and his cowardly brother Godfrey; unscrupulous Tito; swaggering Harold Transome and the over-refined Esther Lyon; swan-necked Rosamond Vincy, susceptible Casaubon; and of course Gwendolen.

The self-absorption of egoism goes hand in hand with an inability or reluctance to see the world from another's viewpoint. 'It never entered into her mind', we're told of Hetty, 'that Adam was pitiable too'; '"whose pain can have been like mine?"', wails Stephen Guest. Because Tom Tulliver considers it an accepted fact that Philip Wakem's father is a rogue, it doesn't occur to him that Philip might be wounded by having the fact pointed out to him. Wriggling from responsibility and blind to the consequences of their actions on others, they show how ruinous the absence of fellow-feeling can be. Some develop a more expansive viewpoint; others don't.

Eliot's egoists aren't caricatures, villains, or anomalies: they demonstrate the human truth that there is no escaping the self. Lest we be too harsh on Tom Tulliver, she reminds us that 'Tom, like every one of us, was imprisoned within the limits of his own nature'. This vision is displayed in one of *Middlemarch*'s famous analogies:

> Your pier-glass or extensive surface of polished steel made to be rubbed by a housemaid, will be minutely and multitudinously scratched in all directions; but place now against it a lighted candle as a centre of illumination, and lo! the scratches will seem to arrange themselves in a fine series of concentric circles round that little sun. It is demonstrable that the scratches are going everywhere impartially, and it is only your candle which produces

the flattering illusion of a concentric arrangement, its light falling with an exclusive optical selection. These things are a parable. The scratches are events, and the candle is the egoism of any person now absent…

We are all the centre of our own universe.

In *Daniel Deronda*, Eliot uses omniscient narration and structure to brilliant effect to pursue this idea. Chapter 16 opens with her own epigraph: 'Men, like planets, have both a visible and an invisible history.' We are only partially legible to others. Grandcourt can read half of Gwendolen's expression of dread, but the other is 'as much out of his imagination as the other side of the moon'. Similarly, when Daniel is out of her orbit, Gwendolen can't conceive that he is being pulled into the gravity of other planets. With a dearth of people to confide in, Gwendolen magnifies their interactions, imagining them to occupy more space in Deronda's mind than they do. The revelation of Daniel's Jewish heritage and engagement to a woman who has existed on the very margins of her consciousness acts like a revolution in both of the word's definitions as an astronomical rotation and an upheaval: she was 'for the first time being dislodged from her supremacy in her own world, and getting a sense that her horizon was but a dipping onward of an existence with which her own was revolving'.

Rather than a structural flaw in the novel, the way Eliot steers a parallel narrative in which Gwendolen's and Daniel's plots barely converge is a formal equivalent of this insight. Long-standing complaints that Eliot cheats the reader by not finally uniting Gwendolen and Daniel (as indeed their own families expect) miss the point Eliot is making: we want the novel, like the world, to be arranged to suit our tastes, but the world was not created for our convenience. Our narrative frustration is egotistical petulance.

The very language we use is saturated with self. As she writes in *Silas Marner*, even a well-meant word of comfort given to those in need gets 'adulterated, in spite of ourselves, before it can pass our lips'. We can send our neighbours comfort food, she adds, without giving it 'a flavour of our own egoism; but language is a stream that is almost sure to smack of a mingled soil'. At its worst, egoism is a serious moral flaw (and something Eliot regularly berated herself for), but more often in her novels it is simply the universal condition. She was endlessly fascinated by how our imprisoned selfhood affects how we perceive and interpret the world.

Motive

'The more I think of it the more I agree in what you said that the really great and abiding interest of philosophy is human motive' (IX.227), Eliot wrote to the Oxford theologian Benjamin Jowett in 1878. When St Ogg's society, which has at best a superficial knowledge of Maggie Tulliver, sees her return unmarried from her botched elopement with Stephen, they see a woman who has transgressed. The narrator adds: 'We judge others according to results; how else?—not knowing the processes by which results are arrived at'. Those processes were precisely what novels were equipped to explore.

People, Eliot believed, are infrequently given to scheming; it was fitting that the word 'plot' was applied to stories, since plotting belonged to fictional worlds but rarely real life. Most daily acts, *Impressions of Theophrastus Such* proposes, are 'performed either in unreflecting obedience to custom and routine or from immediate promptings of thought or feeling to execute an immediate purpose'. The auctioneer Mr Riley in *The Mill on the Floss* offers a test case for how personality, social nicety, and the volatility of human interaction produce unpredictable results. Riley ends up developing an emphatic petition for Stelling as the perfect teacher for Tom despite his having no expertise in the matter and no strong reasons for championing Stelling. The narrator comments that men don't 'usually act and speak from distinct motives, with a consciously proposed end in view';

'Plotting covetousness, and deliberate contrivance, in order to compass a selfish end, are nowhere abundant but in the world of the dramatist.' The lawyer Wakem is seen as a villain by Mr Tulliver, but it never enters Wakem's mind to take over his mill until Mrs Tulliver blunderingly asks him not to.

Eliot loved representing moments of choice. Arthur decides to seek Irwine's advice about Hetty only to retreat in the face of a bonhomie which dimly makes him feel that his dilemma can't be all that serious; Maggie floats into an elopement before being faced with a more conscious decision about whether or not to marry Stephen; Godfrey stays silent rather than acknowledge his child and dead wife; Esther puts off making a choice about her inheritance; Bulstrode follows medical orders preserving the life of his blackmailer but doesn't prevent the nurse from giving him the brandy that will probably kill him...

None of these characters scheme. Moral quandaries come to them, and their response often takes the form of a failure to act or choose, which in their minds reduces their share of responsibility. Such occasions illustrate Eliot's law of consequences, but also offer further evidence of the 'self-deluding' nature of mankind. Often, they show the egoist's reliance on a conception of their likely good luck—always a danger in Eliot. Arthur Donnithorne is overly confident 'that he was really such a good fellow at bottom, Providence would not treat him harshly', while Godfrey shows his 'old disposition to rely on chances which might be favourable to him'.

Romola's Tito and *Daniel Deronda*'s Gwendolen are Eliot's richest accounts of the psychology of choice—of motive as the convergence of slow self-justification and rapid responses to the moment. Here too they are led less by what they want than by what they want to avoid—what is unpleasant for Tito and what is dull and ordinary for Gwendolen. These are negative desires, a shirking of the demands of life. Appropriately, they are also Eliot's most fearful characters—instinctively, irrationally afraid.

If Eliot thought of duty as a form of 'patient obedience', then Tito
and Gwendolen represent its antithesis. Their shared tendency to
see life as a game or gamble again entails an avoidance of choice
and means that consequential decisions are made in an instant.
For Tito, motive is the crystallization of predisposition, desire, and
opportunism. Florence's labyrinthine streets are the spatial
analogue of a man following impulse, and he goes further down
the path leading to outright treachery by encountering there 'one
of those lawless moments which come to us all if we have no guide
but desire'. He becomes overtaken by a kind of id: 'there are
moments when our passions speak and decide for us, and we seem
to stand by and wonder'. Gwendolen too operates without design,
acting on instinctual responses to people and events. Her choices
are as unpredictable as a ball on a roulette wheel: 'she did not
know on which she should fall'. Subconscious sensations provoke
decisions: a drab railway station pushes her towards choosing a
life of luxury that would exclude drab railway stations.

The masterly portrayal of Gwendolen extends the exploration of
what Eliot calls in that novel the 'unmapped country within us'.
Daniel doesn't know who he is legally or culturally, but it's
Gwendolen who is gripped by a sense of her very being as
unknowable and unpredictable: she 'could not foresee what at a
given moment she might like to do'. *Middlemarch* is about knowing
what you want and not getting it; *Daniel Deronda* is about not
knowing what you want. Even the narrator is contaminated by
uncertainty: 'Perhaps' a certain mood had come over Gwendolen
one morning; 'perhaps she was unconsciously finding some of
that mental enlargement'. There is an abundance of compound
words in this most self-aware of novels in which the self works
against the self as often as it strains for mastery: self-abhorrence,
self-blame, self-committal, self-complacent, self-confidence,
self-condemnation, self-consciousness, self-contentment,
self-delight, self-distrust, self-dread, self-exultation, self-lacerating,
self-loving, self-martyring, self-nullification, self-possession,
self-presentation, self-punishment, self-recognition, self-repression,

self-reproach, self-satisfaction, self-suppression, self-suspicion, and more.

The twists and turns of motive meant that there was no guarantee a character would behave consistently. Victorian reviewers expected such consistency—their indignant rejection of Maggie Tulliver's elopement was predicated on their sense that she was acting against her nature—but Eliot fought for the complexity of fictional character. Shakespeare had Macbeth ask: 'Who can be wise, amazed, temperate and furious | Loyal and neutral in a moment?' In *Daniel Deronda*, Eliot responded:

> Macbeth's rhetoric about the impossibility of being many opposite things in the same moment, referred to the clumsy necessities of action and not to the subtler possibilities of feeling. We cannot speak a loyal word and be meanly silent; we cannot kill and not kill in the same moment; but a moment is room wide enough for the loyal and mean desire, for the outlash of a murderous thought and the sharp backward stroke of repentance.

Action might be singular, but feelings are multiple; a plot can be linear, but character is not.

Meaning

'I love words', a 21-year-old Eliot gushed to her friend Maria Lewis; 'they are the quoits, the bows, the staves that furnish the gymnasium of the mind' (I.107–8). In her fiction, she explores how language acts on us and each other, shaping meaning as well as expressing it. In *The Mill on the Floss*, she lingers on the language Stelling uses to think about the educational model he puts Tom through:

> Mr Stelling concluded that Tom's brain, being peculiarly impervious to etymology and demonstrations, was peculiarly in need of being ploughed and harrowed by these patent implements; it was his

favourite metaphor, that the classics and geometry constituted that culture of the mind which prepared it for the reception of any subsequent crop....It is astonishing what a different result one gets by changing the metaphor! Once call the brain an intellectual stomach, and one's ingenious conception of the classics and geometry as ploughs and harrows seems to settle nothing.

The idea of culture, by chain of association, has blended in Stelling's mind with agriculture to produce a theory of learning which he comes to believe in as a fact rather than an interpretation. Tom, as a result, is harrowed in a very different sense. Had Stelling landed on a different metaphor, the outcome for Tom might not necessarily have been better but it would have been different, just as historical images of the mind as a mirror or a lamp affected how early 19th-century poets thought about the imagination.

Eliot 'makes us pleasantly alive to the force of words upon the actors in her story', one contemporary reviewer astutely remarked. In *Middlemarch*, words are a semi-conscious moral choice: Mr Vincy is pleased to hit on the word 'demise' to consider his brother-in-law's death: 'demise' makes the death feel like a legal rather than emotive matter, and so Mr Vincy can enjoy his evening without having to pretend he's sad. 'The right word is always a power, and communicates its definiteness to our action', the narrator comments. Casaubon, conversely, is not released but trapped by language. He had imagined that his 'long studious bachelorhood had stored up for him a compound interest of enjoyment', but Dorothea is a woman rather than a financial investment. '[W]e all of us, grave or light', Eliot warns, 'get our thoughts entangled in metaphors, and act fatally on the strength of them.'

Language is social as well as personal, and she had a taste for representing gatherings in which opinions clash. The best known of these takes place in chapter 6 of *Silas Marner* when Raveloe inhabitants gather round the fire inside the Rainbow Inn. The conversation revolves around four debates: whether the red Durham cow bought by the butcher is the same one previously treated by the farrier; whether the deputy clerk can sing; whether the Lammeters' marriage can be legal if the rector made a grammatical error during the service; and whether ghosts exist in the Lammeter stables. Each time, the landlord seeks compromise: 'The truth lies atween you; you're both right and both wrong, as I allays say.' Eliot doesn't endorse him: she knows that a single cow can't multiply, and his refusal to land on one side comes down partly to habit and partly to his notion of a landlord's necessary neutrality. Even so, her own tendency lies in the direction of multiplicity: 'I protest against any absolute conclusion', she declares in *Middlemarch*, echoing Montaigne's sceptical suspension of judgement.

The exchange of opinions also intrigued her as she knew that everyone gives words a slightly different meaning depending on sociological and psychological contexts and the unique flavour of their egoism. She mentions in 'The Natural History of German Life' that our different experiences cannot but affect 'the picture-writing of the mind'. The word 'railway', for instance, would evoke something different to a navvy, an engineer, a traveller, a railway shareholder, someone who had never been on a train, or even seen one. It was inevitable, then, that our perceptions of the world should diverge. 'Signs are small measurable things, but interpretations are illimitable', she writes in *Middlemarch*. David Carroll sees Eliot as a novelist committed to exploring hermeneutics and highlights the pattern in her novels whereby the shared beliefs of a community are subjected to 'a series of sudden dislocations which makes them reject and revise their ways of looking at the world'.

These ways also include how we account for strange events through superstition, which exists on the boundary of personal and shared beliefs. Lots are drawn by a Nonconformist religious sect to determine Silas Marner's guilt, and Nancy Lammeter interprets natural phenomena like rain as a Heaven-sent sign that she should abandon shopping at a particular place. This interest in superstition had caused difficulties in her first novel. Adam Bede associates a noise with that of a willow wand striking the door, a sound his mother taught him to think of as a portent of death. Unbeknownst to him, Adam's father is indeed dying. Reviewing the novel, John Chapman called this 'supernatural incident' a 'disfigurement'. For him, Eliot had broken the realist contract for the sake of a needlessly implausible detail. Eliot was adamant that this was entirely consistent with realism, since she wasn't saying that the sound and the death were indeed linked but that the association is an interpretative tool used by the character, credible in its context and an expression of genuine peasant culture.

She was sufficiently worried that others would misunderstand her too, though, to risk a more serious disfigurement by asking her publisher to revise future editions. Blackwood acceded to her request and so later editions include a clumsy clarification: 'I tell it as he told it, not attempting to reduce it to its natural elements: in our eagerness to explain impressions, we often lose our hold of the sympathy that comprehends them.' The passage grumbles about the need for explanations even as it offers one, as Eliot had found herself entangled not in metaphor but in the slippery nature of interpretation.

Maxims

Eliot's characters want explanations for a mysterious world. Life feels entirely 'puzzling' to Tulliver and bafflingly 'vague' for Silas Marner. Her women, lacking a proper education, hunger for the explanations they imagine others might possess. Virginia Woolf's father, the critic Leslie Stephen, jokingly referred to Eliot's 'woman in need of a confessor' motif. He has a point. Her female characters often turn to men whom they assume must be better equipped to provide them with answers. Esther looks to Felix for moral illumination, Gwendolen to Deronda, and in both cases the novel rather awkwardly approves the expansion of sympathies that ensues from their admiration.

The outcome is less happy for those women already in possession of a strongly sympathetic nature. Dorothea naively believes that 'The really delightful marriage must be that where your husband was a sort of father, and could teach you even Hebrew, if you wished it'. Romola expects to marry someone rather like Casaubon—a serious scholar—but finds her young, shallow husband equally disappointing. Craving a 'valid law' to follow, she finds a different guide in Savonarola but, being human, the Dominican friar is also flawed and erring. Maggie Tulliver too is desperate for 'some key that would enable her to understand, and, in understanding, endure, the heavy weight that had fallen on her young heart'. With relief, she finds in the works of the 15th-century German-Dutch canon Thomas à Kempis an 'unquestioned message'. This should ring alarm bells: for Eliot, all messages are questionable.

Other characters are led astray by a misguided confidence in their own cognitive abilities. *Middlemarch* depicts two researchers, Casaubon and Lydgate, who have both embarked on impossible, overreaching projects. Casaubon, like Maggie, looks for a key, in his case 'the Key to all Mythologies', which will show 'that all the mythical systems or erratic mythical fragments in the world were corruptions of a tradition originally revealed'. Lydgate strives to identify the 'primitive tissue' from which all tissues in a living organism originate. They are doomed to fail, partly because, as with a poorly titled essay, they've set up their enquiry in slightly the wrong terms. They rely on deductive methods and grope their way to a predetermined outcome. Heuristic methods, the reliance on experience and trial-and-error, would have given them a better chance of recalibrating their quests.

While Casaubon and Lydgate recall Matthew Arnold's characterization in *Culture and Anarchy* of men with a 'staunch adherence to some fixed law of doing', Dorothea becomes increasingly attracted to Will Ladislaw, who exhibits an Arnoldian 'free play' of the mind. Tellingly, Will is so far from sharing Casaubon's and Lydgate's interests in origins that '"he said he should prefer not to know the sources of the Nile"'. (It is tempting to see here an allusion to Samuel Johnson's 18th-century fable *Rasselas*, in which an overambitious attempt to 'trace the Nile through all his passage' similarly collapses, as do the formulaic answers Prince Rasselas is given during his search for the solution to human happiness.) Will may be going too far: disinterestedness comes with its own dangers.

Nonetheless, Eliot's wariness of systematic thinking, the value she placed on tolerance, and the conviction that all human guides are fallible, led to a deep-seated distrust of simplifying, inflexible, and totalizing responses to human behaviour. This is put most strongly in *The Mill on the Floss*:

> All people of broad, strong sense have an instinctive repugnance to the man of maxims; because such people early discern that the mysterious complexity of our life is not to be embraced by maxims, and that to lace ourselves up in formulas of that sort is to repress all the divine promptings and inspirations that spring from growing insight and sympathy.

Rigid maxims are set against a responsive encounter with the world. The word 'sense' privileges inductive reasoning to a deductive intelligence relying on abstraction. Unlike the prefabricated wisdom of a maxim, 'sense' (which combines the cerebral and the felt) is instinctive. To 'discern' is also to perceive and discriminate in a way that is reactive. To the fixity of the narrow maxim, Eliot opposes the breadth and movement of the insight that grows.

The dangers of rigid thinking are an enduring theme in Eliot, there from the start of her career—indeed, of her life, having been subjected to the inflexible character her brother Isaac shared with Tom Tulliver. 'Generalities are the refuge at once of deficient intellectual activity and deficient feeling', she warned in an astonishing demolition of the 18th-century poet Edward Young. In *Scenes of Clerical Life*, she worries about 'that facile psychology which prejudges individuals by means of formulæ'; in *Romola*, Bardo's 'lip-born maxims were as powerless over the passion which had been moving him' as a good-luck charm; in *Daniel Deronda*, while men are drawn to 'axioms, definitions, and propositions', 'No formulas for thinking will save us mortals from mistake in our imperfect apprehension of the matter to be thought about'.

Eliot clung to 'the truth', voiced in *The Mill on the Floss*, 'that moral judgments must remain false and hollow, unless they are checked and enlightened by a perpetual reference to the special circumstances that mark the individual lot'. The genre of the novel, which deals with the trajectories of individuals and stays close to particulars, is well suited to express that truth. If her sentences can sometimes read as tortuous or convoluted, it is because she believes in the value of questioning our most facile and comfortable interpretations. 'But I check myself', a paragraph in *Impressions of Theophrastus Such* begins. Eliot's habitual self-checking affected the way she lived and the way she wrote; it operates as a mode of return and revision practised by her characters—physically, psychologically, morally—and syntactically by the narrator.

Sensing

Cognition in Eliot's novels is bodily as well as rational. Sense includes sensation; to feel is to experience an emotion but also to touch or respond to physical stimulus. Her views on the subject were shaped by her intimate knowledge of another philosopher.

Had Lewes not bungled the publication negotiations, Eliot would have had yet another claim to fame as the first translator of Spinoza's *Ethics* into English. Her work, completed in 1856, wasn't published until 1981. Regardless, she was part of the astonishing mid-19th-century revival in fortunes of the 17th-century atheistical Jewish philosopher whose works had long been ignored in England.

Whereas Western philosophy had long maintained the dualism of mind and body, Spinoza's monism made them part of the same being: 'Thought' and 'Extension' existing in parallel but not separate states, with neither superior to the other. He went further, locating the origin of mental perception within the body: 'For the mind does not know itself except so far as it perceives ideas of the affections of the body.'

Spinoza's ideas about cognition relate to Eliot's in at least two other ways. Like her, he knew that the physiological nature of perception complicated ideas about realism, since humans aren't capable of perceiving an objective reality. In fact, Eliot's musings about subjective responses to the word railway is one most likely borrowed from Spinoza, who had offered his own (historically available) example of a horse. A soldier seeing the 'footsteps of a horse in the sand' will associate the thought with a rider and, from that, to the idea of war, 'But a rustic will pass from the thought of a horse to that of a plough, of a field, etc': and so each individual 'will have this or that succession of ideas'. Spinoza also believed that 'the individuals composing the human body, and consequently the human body itself, is affected by external bodies in a variety of modes'. As the philosopher and biographer Clare Carlisle nicely captures, 'Spinozism is a philosophy of encounter and transformation, not of solid substances and fixed essences'. This would also be a good summary of Eliot's fiction.

She had further strong reasons to be preoccupied with how we know the world through our bodily frames: this was the subject of

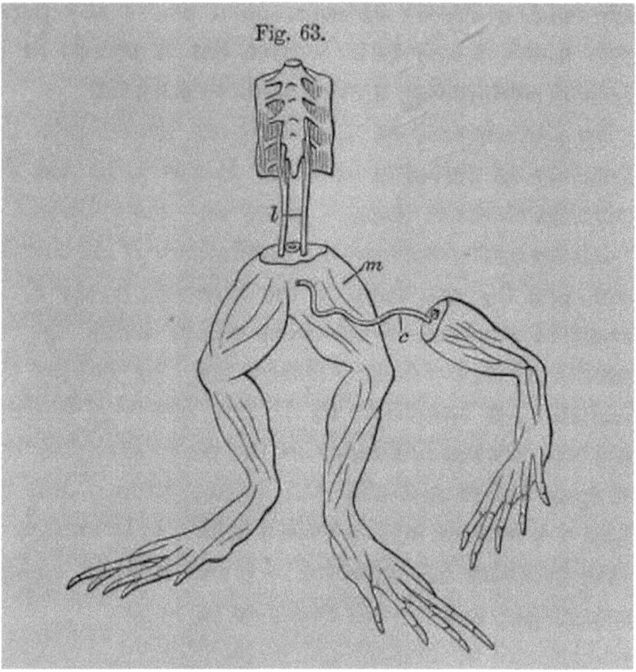

Fig. 63.

6. Diagram of a frog's nerves connected to another frog, from the chapter 'Our Senses and Sensations' in George Henry Lewes's *The Physiology of Common Life* (1859–60), demonstrating 'those manifold streams of sensation which make up our general Consciousness' (II, 287–8). Lewes was evidently continuing his experiments on frogs in 1867, when Eliot added a postscript (crossed out) to a letter: 'Froggie continues to do better than even he expected without his head *brain* for months. He dies of starvation at last' (*Letters*, IV.405).

Lewes's scientific research for much of their life together (Figure 6). (One early biographer describes the frogs Lewes kept for his studies occasionally jumping into their dining-room.) As Eliot embarked on her career as a novelist, Lewes was completing *The Physiology of Common Life*, published the same year as *Adam Bede*. The former object of Eliot's affections, Herbert Spencer, also shared these interests and had already published his *Principles of Psychology* four years earlier. The surge in physiological research in the 1850s also counted Alexander Bain's studies *The Senses and the Intellect* and *The Emotions and the Will*. Spinoza's philosophy chimed in many ways with their research—he was useful for scientists committed to testing the hypothesis that we understand the world through our muscles, our nerves, our skin—and many of them (Lewes in particular) championed his ideas in England.

Lewes believed that mental phenomena were closely linked to the body's nervous structure. It was Lewes who first coined the phrase 'stream of consciousness' to describe the unconscious impressions made on us by surrounding sounds or smells—drawing, strikingly, on the sound of a mill-wheel to make his point. He concluded: 'The reader's daily experience will assure him that over and above all the particular sensations capable of being separately recognised, there is a general stream of Sensation which constitutes his feeling of existence—the Consciousness of himself as a sensitive being.'

Eliot's characters are sensitive beings. They 'quiver', 'shiver', and 'tremble'; they experience 'electric shocks'; their 'fibres' are stirred. These are moments of cognition. A feeling can be an idea, an emotion, or a sensation; in Eliot, the three often combine to produce shifts in consciousness. In *Scenes of Clerical Life*, Caterina plays the harpsichord:

> The vibration rushed through Caterina like an electric shock: it seemed as if at that instant a new soul were entering into her, and filling her with a deeper, more significant life.

Her characters don't think: they vibrate. Grasping—hands, objects—matter in the novels. Her deep interest in orators—the Methodist preacher Dinah Morris, the friar Savonarola, the 'radical' Felix Holt—speaks to her fascination with how individuals can transform one another through fellow-feeling but also through physiological responses to the timbre of a particular voice. In *The Mill on the Floss*, we know Philip's love for Maggie is hopeless the instant we are told his voice is 'high, feeble', in contrast with Stephen's 'fine bass'.

Human susceptibility to external influence is of course not without its dangers. Maggie is powerfully responsive to music (as Eliot herself was) and feels 'her soul was being played on in this way by the inexorable power of sound'. Her later elopement with Stephen is something she doesn't initially choose but drifts into, partly lulled by 'the delicious rhythmic dip of the oars', prompting Stephen to insist that an event that '"has come upon us without our seeking"' mitigates their culpability. More often, however, bodily responses are a surer guide to truth than the more supposedly rational acts of self-persuasion. The instinctive chills and shivers Maggie experiences in relation to the idea of her engagement to Philip are the language of her subconscious, just as Romola's shuddering response to the discovery that her husband secretly wears armour communicates his cowardice to her before her strong sense of marital duty permits her to recognize Tito's moral failures more explicitly.

Indeed, Eliot might well have agreed with Keats that 'axioms in philosophy are not axioms until they are proved upon our pulses'. Her focus on bodily responses relates to her distaste for the ethical limitations of men of maxims and the aesthetic limitations of the diagram: both are too abstract, too theoretical, too entirely rational. As the narrator puts it in *Middlemarch*:

> We are all of us born in moral stupidity, taking the world as an udder to feed our supreme selves: Dorothea had early begun to emerge from that stupidity, but yet it had been easier to her to imagine how she would devote herself to Mr Casaubon, and become wise and strong in his strength and wisdom, than to conceive with that distinctness which is no longer reflection but feeling—an idea

wrought back to the directness of sense, like the solidity of
objects—that he had an equivalent centre of self, whence the lights
and shadows must always fall with a certain difference.

This single sentence performs astonishing variations of
perspective. Dorothea's first tentative departure from egoism leads
her into fresh difficulties because, at first, the other person is still
only experienced as an idea, and one that will ultimately serve the
self. Her imaginings are a projection, a story of which she remains
the heroine. Free-floating speculation must be checked by tangible
knowledge so that an idea can become a truth. Eliot hoped that
we too would experience—would feel—her novels so that we could
access that truth.

Chapter 5
Meliorism

What would encountering George Eliot's novels have been like for her original readers? As modern readers, it's hard for us to recapture at least three things. We miss what it would have been like to live with *Romola*, *Middlemarch*, and *Daniel Deronda* over a year or more, experiencing the slow unfolding of her wide-ranging plots. Eliot often refers to her characters as having a 'history', and the care with which she shows the various factors that slowly build them over time was accompanied by the incremental publication of her later works.

We also tend to forget that for her first readers, as for us, the novels were historical novels, set in periods more or less remote from them. If we mark the beginning of the Victorian period as 1837, when Queen Victoria came to the throne, then only *Daniel Deronda* is a Victorian novel, and even that takes place a decade before it was published. The others are set during Eliot's youth (the late 1820s and early 1830s, when much of *Scenes of Clerical Life*, *The Mill on the Floss*, part of *Silas Marner*, *Felix Holt*, and *Middlemarch* are set), or her father's youth (the late 18th century and early 19th century, when 'Mr Gilfil's Love-Story', much of *Adam Bede*, and the early sections of *Silas Marner* are set). In the case of *Romola* she goes back as far as the 15th century.

And finally, we may forget that, if Eliot's language can sometimes sound foreign to us, it often sounded strange to them too. The critic Sidney Colvin put it best when he reviewed *Middlemarch*:

> She has walked between two epochs, upon the confines of two worlds, and has described the old in terms of the new. To the old world belong the elements of her experience, to the new world the elements of her reflection on experience.... Thus there is the most pointed contrast between the matter of these English tales and the manner of their telling. The matter is antiquated in our recollections, the manner seems to anticipate the future of our thoughts.

The realism with which she represents the lives of clergymen, dairy farmers, schoolchildren, and provincial young women is coupled with a narrative commentary shot through with the most cutting-edge philosophical and scientific ideas. Evolutionary language runs through *The Mill on the Floss*. The famous Rainbow Inn scene in *Silas Marner*, another contemporary critic perceived, brings together rustic matter ('unintellectual social life') with a far-from-rustic manner (a 'strong intellectual impress').

Some readers were bothered by the modern jargon which seemed to drive a wedge between the perspective of Eliot's characters and that of her narrators. However, the effect it generates feeds what Eliot has to say about change. The novels aren't just set in the past: they want to draw attention to the gap between past and present. She takes readers back, as in *Adam Bede*, to 'old leisurely times, when the boat, gliding sleepily along the canal, was the newest locomotive wonder', in contrast to the present when 'Leisure is gone—gone where the spinning-wheels are gone, and the pack-horses, and the slow waggons'. 'Mr Gilfil's Love-Story' evokes a period 25 years earlier, before gas-light and commuters travelling home on the new railway line that would also come for Middlemarchers. (The Nuneaton railway line opened in 1847.)

Silas Marner and Mirah Cohen both search urban streets for a building from their past, only to find it has been torn down.

The spiritual and intellectual chasm would have been, if anything, more dizzying still. The novelist and biographer J. A. Froude was born a year before Eliot and, like her, found his religious faith shaken. The 1849 novel in which he expressed his doubts, *The Nemesis of Faith*, was publicly burned in Oxford, where he lost his fellowship. From the vantage point of the 1880s, just as Oscar Wilde was setting off on his American lecture tour to preach aestheticism, Froude looked back at what it had been like for his and Eliot's generation to live through the first half of the 19th century, an era of 'swift if silent spiritual revolution', of political reform, religious doubt, technological innovation, and educational change:

> Thus all round us, the intellectual lightships had broken from their moorings, and it was then a new and trying experience. The present generation which has grown up in an open spiritual ocean, which has got used to it and has learned to swim for itself, will never know what it was to find the lights all drifting, the compasses all awry, and nothing left to steer by except the stars.

Memory

In addition to nausea-inducing headaches, Eliot suffered from depression. She kept a journal in which she tracked her poor health and the progress of her writing—the latter regularly interrupted by the former. The journal entries were props. She could read back old entries and recall what she lost sight of whenever she was gripped by despair: that she had felt like this before and had come out the other side. 'It is worth while to record my great depression of spirits, that I may remember one more resurrection from the pit of melancholy', she wrote in the midst of a particularly grim episode. Later she documented: 'I have often been helped by looking back in it to compare former with actual states of despondency from bad health or other apparent causes. In this way a past despondency has turned to present hopefulness.'

In the novels, pain is acute for those who have nothing to compare it with and no memory of having previously survived it. This accounts for the intensity of childhood sorrow even in the face of seemingly trivial events, as she paints so vividly in *The Mill on the Floss*, and of our first heartbreak, as in *Adam Bede*:

> For there is no despair so absolute as that which comes with the first moments of our first great sorrow, when we have not yet known what it is to have suffered and be healed, to have despaired and to have recovered hope.

Eliot's ideas about memory are often Wordsworthian and echo his understanding in *The Prelude* that 'feeling comes in aid | Of feeling, and diversity of strength | Attends us, if but once we have been strong'.

Her focus on 'local attachments' is also Wordsworthian, to which she brought an understanding that we need to form bonds with tangible things if we are later to meet the more abstract claims of morality and duty. In *The Mill on the Floss*, Tom leaves school for the Christmas holidays and returns to 'the familiar hearth':

> There is no sense of ease like the ease we felt in those scenes where we were born, where objects became dear to us before we had known the labour of choice, and where the outer world seemed only an extension of our own personality…Very commonplace, even ugly, that furniture of our early home might look if it were put up to auction…and is not the striving after something better and better in our surroundings, the grand characteristic that distinguishes man from the brute…? But heaven knows where that striving might lead us, if our affections had not a trick of twining round those old inferior things—if the loves and sanctities of our life had no deep immovable roots in memory.

In a typical move, the passage checks itself: it reaches forward to a supposedly sophisticated adulthood before turning back. That our earliest bonds are pre-verbal—feelings rather than thoughts—increases their potency for the adult who remembers them. They link us to a time of prelapsarian wholeness (before 'the labour of choice') and build appreciation for the ordinary.

Eliot often returned to this idea that 'We could never have loved the earth so well if we had had no childhood in it'. Gwendolen's impatience with restraints is partly explained on the grounds that she has no childhood home to return to: 'A human life, I think, should be well rooted in some spot of a native land', Eliot comments, adding that 'At five years old, mortals are not prepared to be citizens of the world, to be stimulated by abstract nouns, to soar above preference into impartiality'. We are nourished by what is near and familiar. A sign of Gwendolen's moral growth at the end of the novel is her newfound affection for Offendene, which she secures for her family (Figure 7).

7. **Griff House, where Eliot spent her youth, as it appears in the biography John Walter Cross published soon after her death.**

Froude's description of growing up as an early Victorian is one Eliot would have recognized, but she might have countered that her generation did not only have the stars to steer them: memory was the anchor that could prevent individuals and society from drifting. In *The Mill on the Floss*, Maggie's painful dilemma is between the new ties of romantic love and the older ties of family and friendship. She chooses the past because, as she pleads to Stephen, '"If the past is not to bind us, where can duty lie? We should have no law but the inclination of the moment."' Dr Kenn later reframes her decision more broadly:

> 'Your prompting to go to your nearest friends,—to remain where all the ties of your life have been formed—is a true prompting...At present everything seems tending towards the relaxation of ties,— towards the substitution of wayward choice for the adherence to obligation, which has its roots in the past.'

Although the novel appears to endorse Maggie's choice (to which we are the more easily reconciled because of Stephen's evident shortcomings) it comes at enormous cost for her. The regressive quality of the novel's ending, which sees Maggie and Tom returning to the state of children as they drown, clasped in a final loving embrace, raises more problems than it solves about the potency of past ties to see us through crises.

Eliot rectifies this problem in *Silas Marner*, the novel which makes the strongest case for memory as a redemptive force. Having abandoned the community which has falsely accused him of theft, Silas 'hated the thought of the past; there was nothing that called out his love and fellowship toward the strangers he had come amongst; and the future was all dark'. The discovery of fellowship relies on the recovery of the past. When a neighbour falls ill, he remembers the natural remedies his mother used, and this 'sense of unity between his past and present life, which might have been the beginning of his rescue'. But it is Eppie, who Silas at first mistakes for his long-dead little sister, who provides this unity: 'As the child's mind was growing into knowledge, his mind was growing into memory.'

At the simplest level, sympathy relies on memory. Remembering what it had been like to be falsely accused stops Silas in his tracks when he starts to blame a neighbour for stealing his gold: 'Memory was not so utterly torpid in Silas that it could not be wakened by these words.' Like-for-like experiences would be a fragile foundation for widespread fellow-feeling, however. Eppie's arrival brings Silas into contact with his neighbours: 'By seeking what was needful for Eppie', Silas becomes acquainted with

> the forms of custom and belief which were the mould of Raveloe life; and as, with reawakening sensibilities, memory also reawakened, he had begun to ponder over the elements of his old faith, and blend them with his new impressions, till he recovered a consciousness of unity between his past and present.

What is important about this state of harmony is that change has brought it about. In a novel full of people bursting into rooms and crossing thresholds, Eppie's arrival disrupts a life of routine which has become stagnant. Change that could nurture rather than break past ties was Eliot's ideal.

Politics

'[S]ince you have read my books, you must perceive that the bent of my mind is conservative rather than destructive' (IV.472), Eliot wrote to the physician Clifford Allbutt. This would indeed have been abundantly clear to anyone following her career. The first words of her first story express nostalgia for Shepperton Church as it appeared 25 years ago, and admits to a 'tenderness' for the 'crumbling, picturesque inefficiency' that the 'spick-and-span new-painted, new-varnished efficiency' was doing away with. (A smug sense that modern ways are an improvement on old practices is almost always met with sarcasm in the novels.)

Her final work, *Impressions of Theophrastus Such*, maintains a 'tender attachment' to the landscape of her father's youth, 'helping to unite us pleasantly with the elder generations who tilled the soil for us before we were born'.

It might have been expected that a writer with such strong views about 'the man of maxims' should feel wary of politics. 'I thought you understood', she rebuked a friend in 1878, 'that I have grave reasons for not speaking on certain public topics'. Having acquired a sage-like status, her opinion was sought on matters private and public, but she insisted that her role was that of 'rousing' the 'nobler emotions, which make mankind desire the social right, not the prescribing of special measures' (VII.44). Yet she wrote (or did she?) a political novel. Composed in the run-up to the 1867 Second Reform Act and set shortly after the 1832 first Reform Act, *Felix Holt, the Radical* depicts the events surrounding an election in the fictional town of Treby Magna. Blackwood's reassurance that 'Her politics are excellent and will attract all parties' (IV.247) gives some indication of how seriously one should take the title's epithet.

Felix shares with his creator a profound scepticism about the vote. To her publisher, Eliot declared herself 'no believer in Salvation by Ballot' (VI.21–2). She expressed relief that the campaign for female franchise was stalling: 'that is best, for woman does not yet deserve a much better lot than man gives her' (II.86). Until women were better educated, the vote was 'an extremely doubtful good' (IV.390). Felix's income, like Eliot's sex, disqualifies him from voting, but he's not keen on it anyway. Disenfranchisement doesn't stop him from holding forth: 'It's another sort of power that I want us working men to have, and I can see plainly enough that our all having votes will do little towards it at present.' Again, access to political power without the educational and moral changes that would enable power to be used to good effect is precisely the kind of sudden change that makes both Eliot and Felix nervous. For the latter, until the working classes could '"show there's something they love better than swilling themselves with ale, extension of the suffrage can never mean anything for them but extension of boozing"'.

Surprisingly, Eliot accepted Blackwood's invitation that she publish a spin-off article written in the voice of Felix Holt for *Blackwood's Edinburgh Magazine*. 'Address to Working Men, by Felix Holt' appeared in January 1868. It makes use of the widespread 19th-century image of the body politic ('society stands before us like that wonderful piece of life, the human body, with all its various parts depending on one another') and cautions against dismantling old structures to make way for new. Felix preaches: 'it would be fool's work to batter down a pump only because a better might be made, when you had no machinery ready for a new one'. The speech reminds one of Eliot's approval of the historian Riehl, a man who arrived at a 'social-political-conservatism' more philosophical than political. This description fits her too, as does Riehl's belief that 'What has grown up historically can only die out historically, by the gradual operation of necessary laws'.

Like so many Victorian novelists who had grown up in the shadow of the French Revolution and nervously seen the 1848 Revolutions spread across the Channel, Eliot felt compelled to represent crowds. Almost too much in *Romola*, in which barely a day seems to go by in 15th-century Florence without its designated carnival, but such scenes allowed her to depict the tangled web of individual impulses and collective energies that captivated her. Her treatment of the riot in *Felix Holt*, in which members of a mob imagine that there might be a clearer overarching motive to the riots which they can't perceive, prompts the comment that 'It was that mixture of pushing forward and being pushed forward, which is a brief history of most human things'. Mob scenes are not, however, Eliot's forte, and the cursory fashion in which she deals with Felix's manslaughter of a constable is possibly the most egregious betrayal of her aesthetic and moral values in her works.

Eliot is better when she shows how the changing industrial and political landscape of the 1830s was making communities more interdependent than ever before and on a broader canvas. Treby Magna was passing

> from being simply a respectable market-town—the heart of a great rural district, where the trade was only such as had close relations with the local landed interest—and took on the more complex life brought by mines and manufactures, which belong more directly to the great circulating system of the nation than to the local system to which they had been superadded.

Here she rehearses her later description of Middlemarch at a time when 'Municipal town and rural parish gradually made fresh threads of connexion—gradually, as the old stocking gave way to the savings-bank'. The modern expansion of previously local webs to a national, even international, scale produced ambivalence in Eliot. She was herself profoundly cosmopolitan, and new connections—with places and people—were conduits of the new perspectives she associated with moral growth. But she was also always nervous about the loss of tangible good that might come with large-scale thinking.

Instead, her characters continue to find scope for meaningful acts on a small, local scale. When Felix decides to '"make life less bitter for a few within my reach"', he pre-empts Dorothea's belief that '"we have no right to come forward and urge wider changes for good, until we have tried to alter the evils which lie under our own hands"'. Genius, Eliot proposes in *Middlemarch*, consists in 'a power to make or do, not anything in general, but something in particular'. In an essay on the feminist writers Mary Wollstonecraft and Margaret Fuller, she argued that

> There is a perpetual action and reaction between individuals and institutions; we must try and mend both by little and little—the only way in which human things can be mended.

She suggested, in 1877, that she had found her own word for this: 'I don't know that I ever heard anybody use the word "meliorist" except myself.' Characteristically, she instantly qualified the claim: 'But I begin to think that there is no good invention or discovery that has not been made by more than one person' (VI.333). (She was right: the *OED* dates the word to 1846.)

Heroism

In her early fiction like *Adam Bede*, Eliot pushed aside 'prophets, sibyls, and heroic warriors' for commonplace men and women, because there 'are few prophets in the world; few sublimely beautiful women; few heroes'. But starting with *Romola*—a novel which contains prophets and a sublimely beautiful woman—she became more interested in exploring the parameters within which heroic action was possible. If Tito is the closest Eliot ever came to writing a villain, then Romola is the nearest she came to portraying a heroine, or indeed a saint. After her godfather's execution, Romola drifts away from Florence on a boat that leads her to a village ravaged by the plague. Rather than running from the survivors, she tends them fearlessly.

The awe Romola inspires is increased by the nun's costume she assumed to escape Florence: she is to the villagers a Madonna, the '"Holy Mother, come to take care of the people who have the pestilence"', the 'sweet and sainted Lady with her fair face, her golden hair, and her brown eyes that had a blessing in them'. Gradually, she breathes life back into the village and 'legends were afterwards told in that valley about the blessed Lady who came over the sea', and 'had done beautiful loving deeds there, rescuing those who were ready to perish'. Her heroism invokes Christ as well as Mary. It involves determining 'where the sacredness of obligation ended and where the sacredness of rebellion began'. Needing to find a role for herself outside the institutions of marriage, State, and Church, Romola discovers that the heroic act is as much one of self-creation as one of charity (Figure 8).

8. Frederic Leighton illustrated *Romola*, the only one of Eliot's novels to originally appear with images. Here, the Madonna-like Romola comes to the aid of a plague-stricken community.

Romola doesn't feel herself to be particularly heroic. Those who do feel heroic, as Arthur Donnithorne does as he strides towards his stables, rarely are. Romola briefly conceives that she might lead a lonely life in a state of 'proud stoical heroism', but true heroism in Eliot is anything but proud. When Romola acts most generously and selflessly, as when she sets out to find and rescue her husband's mistress and children, 'She never for a moment told herself that it was heroism or exalted charity in her to seek these beings.' Mostly, Eliot's characters think of heroism as something that exists somewhere else: in other people (like Savonarola) or in another epoch. The notion of heroism, for the Machiavellian Tito, is used as a jibe, the sign of someone forgetting their time, their place, their genre: 'you will have surpassed all the heroines of the Greek drama', he sneers at his wife.

Eliot thought about the ever-receding perspective of the heroic. For Romola, growing up in 15th-century Florence with a pagan father, heroism lies in the classical past. She had been accustomed to think of heroic deeds and great principles as something antithetic to the vulgar present, of the Pnyx and the Forum as something more worthy of attention than the councils of living Florentine men.

But *Romola*, as the Proem makes clear and as reviewers immediately saw, was full of resonance for readers of the 1860s. In *Impressions of Theophrastus Such*, she also dwells on the tendency the Victorians shared with Romola of only seeing greatness in the remote past—perhaps, in their case, in Romola's 15th-century Italy: 'the period thus looked back on with a purely admiring regret, as perfect enough to suit a superior mind, is always a long way off; the desirable contemporaries are hardly nearer than Leonardo da Vinci'. We aren't used to thinking about what's near as being grand: 'Three-quarters of a century ago is not a distance that lends much enchantment to the view.'

But people don't fundamentally change. '[W]e still resemble the men of the past more than we differ from them', *Romola*'s proem insists;

> we are impressed with the broad sameness of the human lot, which never alters in the main headings of its history—hunger and labour, seed-time and harvest, love and death.

Eliot doesn't collapse all distinctions: certain socio-historical conditions are of course more or less propitious for certain kinds of actions. The Prelude of *Middlemarch* addresses this. The 'passionate, ideal nature' of the 16th-century Spanish reformer Teresa of Avila 'demanded an epic life', but 'later-born Theresas were helped by no coherent social faith and order which could perform the function of knowledge for the ardently willing soul'. A 19th-century woman would find it hard to express her ideals and yearnings as Theresa did without being 'disapproved' or 'condemned'.

In *Daniel Deronda*, Eliot's only novel set in the Victorian period, she lingered on the idea. Was the 19th century intrinsically unpropitious for heroism, or is it that we don't recognize heroism when we see it up close? For Matthew Arnold, the 18th century was famously 'the age of prose', but life as a Victorian also felt insistently prosaic—prosaic as in dull and commonplace, and prosaic in that it looked for its narratives in the novel rather than epic, drama, or even poetry. Eliot gets mileage out of the strange contrast between the visionary Mordecai, spiritually equipped for epic, and his surroundings. When Daniel arranges more suitable lodgings for Mordecai before reuniting him with his sister Mirah, it's partly to detach him (snobbishly, one might say) from the uncomfortably prosaic pawnbrokers he lives with. The narrator comments: 'In the heroic drama, great recognitions are not encumbered with these details'.

Mordecai's lodging then needs to be furnished:

> Such is the irony of earthly mixtures, that the heroes have not always had carpets and tea-cups of their own; and, seen through the open window by the mackerel-vendor, may have been invited with some hopefulness to pay three hundred per cent in the form of fourpence.

Daniel Deronda is shot through with such strange juxtapositions of the heroic and prosaic. The great men of history would look strange in Victorian England—'We sit up at night to read about Çakya-Mouni, Saint Francis, or Oliver Cromwell; but whether we should be glad for any one at all like them to call on us the next morning' is 'quite another affair'. Eliot is struck by the incongruence of harbouring visionary ideas while dressing for a white tie dinner in the 1860s.

Curiously, whereas Eliot had begun her novelistic career asking readers to find the 'poetry and the pathos' in ordinary life, it's now her own character Daniel, we're told, who has developed the skill to 'easily find poetry and romance among the events of everyday life'. 'And perhaps', the narrator adds, poetry and romance truly 'are as plentiful as ever in the world', existing alongside the mundane Victorian clutter of top hats and train station waiting-rooms. In an 1868 letter, Eliot had written:

> I see clearly that we ought, each of us, not to sit down and wail, but to be heroic and constructive, if possible, like the strong souls who lived before, as in other [eras] of religious decay. (IV.472)

But what did it mean to 'be heroic'?

Hidden lives

'It is interesting, I think, to know whether a writer was born in a central or border district—a condition which always has a strongly determining influence' (VI.163), Eliot wrote in 1875 in answer to an American author's questions. Most of Eliot's fiction draws on the first 30-odd years she spent in what Henry James called 'the core and centre of the English world; midmost England, unmitigated England'.

For her characters who live in a fictionalized Warwickshire, or the Wessex setting of *Daniel Deronda*, major international events barely register. The Austen-like gossip about a new eligible bachelor animating Gwendolen's neighbourhood prompts the un-Austenian commentary:

> Could there be a slenderer, more insignificant thread in human history than this consciousness of a girl, busy with her small inferences of the way in which she could make her life pleasant?—in a time, too, when ideas were with fresh vigour making armies of themselves, and the universal kinship was declaring itself fiercely: when women on the other side of the world would not mourn for the husbands and sons who died bravely in a common cause, and men stinted of bread on our side of the world heard of that willing loss and were patient.

The American civil war is suddenly, abruptly brought into the orbit of the reader's consciousness. Eliot's novels often built in allusions to 19th-century events, but never so starkly as this. Although Eliot so often found value in what seemed insignificant, here the juxtaposition reduces Gwendolen's preoccupations to the level of mock-epic. And, as if consequential acts were now only possible far away from modern England, the novel ends with Daniel leaving for the Middle East.

Eliot often made use of large perspectival shifts, but the turn to global events was more recent. Daniel's departure represents a striking change for a novelist who had more often worried about how the pull exerted by global concerns might risk a dispersal of energies. Brooke's political speeches in *Middlemarch* satirize such a diffuseness:

> 'We must look all over the globe:—"Observation with extensive view," must look everywhere, "from China to Peru," as somebody says—Johnson, I think, "The Rambler," you know. That is what I have done up to a certain point—not as far as Peru; but I've not always stayed at home—I saw it wouldn't do.'

His sentences are as incomplete as his projects, lost beyond the horizon. Such ineffectiveness is a warning of what might happen to the narrator should they also lose focus: 'all the light I can command must be concentrated on this particular web, and not dispersed over that tempting range of relevancies called the universe'.

Earlier, Felix Holt had voiced the terror of wasted energies that Eliot never seemed able to shake:

> 'Not to waste energy, to apply force where it would tell, to do small work close at hand, not waiting for speculative chances of heroism, but preparing for them'—these were the rules he had been constantly urging on himself.

Eliot's women don't have much choice in the matter but to obey these rules: the 'tempting range' of the universe holds little for them. Esther Lyon is baffled by Felix: 'Did he want her to be heroic?', she wonders, insisting to him later that '"A woman can hardly ever choose in that way; she is dependent on what happens to her"'. Gwendolen impatiently reminds Grandcourt that 'We women can't go in search of adventures—to find out the North-West Passage or the source of the Nile'. A clear sense of what 'small good work close at hand' might be, however, eludes them. *Middlemarch* pokes fun at Dorothea's restlessness: 'What was there to be done in the village? Oh dear! nothing. Everybody was well and had flannel; nobody's pig had died.'

As Eliot stretched the boundaries of the genre of tragedy to include insignificant lives, so did she assess whether room could be made for them within the genre of epic. The former is particularly invested in capturing an immediate emotional intensity, and Eliot associates it with our ability to feel. The latter is more concerned with the nature of narrative, of what we leave behind, of the mark we make on history. Eliot wasn't alone in attempting such generic revisionism. For all the Victorians's love of hero-worship, 19th-century historical writing gave new prominence to obscure lives. In 1841, Thomas Carlyle paid tribute to 'The noble silent men, scattered here and there, each in his department; silently thinking, silently working; whom no Morning Newspaper makes mention of!' Thomas Babington Macaulay drew attention to the 'noiseless revolutions' whose 'progress is rarely indicated by what historians are pleased to call important events'. J. R. Green explained in his best-selling *Short History of the English People*, published two years after *Middlemarch*, that, instead of the usual military and political figures, he wanted to 'find a place for figures little heeded in common history'. Eliot combines the sociological emphasis on historical impact (in *Adam Bede* she argues that 'insignificant' people 'affect the price of bread and the rate of wages') with a Carlylean emphasis on tragic nobility.

We first glimpse this in *The Mill on the Floss*. While Tom Tulliver is 'engaged in a dustier, noisier warfare', his sister Maggie endures battles that lie 'almost entirely within her own soul, one shadowy army fighting another'. Eliot adds:

> So it has been since the days of Hecuba, and of Hector, Tamer of
> horses: inside the gates, the women with streaming hair and
> uplifted hands offering prayers, watching the world's combat from
> afar, filling their long, empty days with memories and fears;
> outside, the men, in fierce struggle with things divine and human,
> quenching memory in the stronger light of purpose, losing the
> sense of dread and even of wounds in the hurrying ardour of action.

She summons those Homeric epic similes which briefly flash a light on the plight of women, weeping over their fallen husbands and sons, as when Odysseus cries 'as a woman | weeps, as she falls to wrap her arms around | her husband, fallen fighting for his home | and children'. But their struggle has historic as well as mythic significance: it 'belongs to every historical advance of mankind, is represented in this way in every town, and by hundreds of obscure hearths'.

Epic stayed on her mind in *Middlemarch*, where she resists the tendency to assume that, because novels so often end in marriage, marriage is a terminus. Marriage, she objects, 'is still the beginning of the home epic'. Adam and Eve's story truly begins after their 'honeymoon in Eden', when they enter the world and therefore history. Eliot is aware that honouring the home epic requires another perspectival inversion. The novel opens with Dorothea looking for significance, for a sphere in which '"There would be nothing trivial about our lives. Every-day things with us would mean the greatest things."' The novel's Finale meets that hope.

Eliot's tribute to Dorothea and future Dorotheas, perhaps the most beloved passage in all of Eliot's works, closes *Middlemarch*:

Her finely-touched spirit had still its fine issues, though they were not widely visible. Her full nature, like that river of which Cyrus broke the strength, spent itself in channels which had no great name on the earth. But the effect of her being on those around her was incalculably diffusive: for the growing good of the world is partly dependent on unhistoric acts; and that things are not so ill with you and me as they might have been, is half owing to the number who lived faithfully a hidden life, and rest in unvisited tombs.

If this ending feels so affirming yet at the same time so melancholy, it is perhaps because it's poised between loss and gain. 'Home epic' is again shadowed by myth and history. The Greek historian Herodotus told the tale of the Persian king Cyrus who diverted, and thereby weakened, the gushing river Gyndes in retribution for the drowning of his horse. The narrator's expansive vision irrigates the narrow stream of Dorothea's hidden life with grandeur, but even as Eliot stresses Dorothea's generative influence, the passage, with its 'un-' prefixes, is shadowed by a sense of waste.

Despite Eliot's agnosticism, these lines are often read at funerals both religious and secular. They seem poised between those too. A few months after Eliot's death, a Jesuit writer who, like Eliot, was given to depression, undertook a thirty-day Long Retreat. Contemplating what might remain of his, or any, obscure life, he pondered the example of Jesus:

the hidden life at Nazareth is the great help to faith for us who must live more or less an obscure, constrained, and unsuccessful life … What was his life there?—One of devotion … also one of labour; and of obedience: in every way it looked ordinary, presented *nothing* that could attract the world, not even austerities like those of St John in the wilderness.

Gerard Manley Hopkins's name, like Eliot's, has not disappeared. Their beliefs were very different, but it is hard to imagine that Eliot, who for the first book she ever wrote reluctantly separated the myth of Jesus's life from the naked historical facts, would have bristled at the parallel.

Chapter 6
Afterlife

John Walter Cross had hoped his wife might be buried in a much-visited tomb. Shortly after she died of kidney disease on 22 December 1880, aged only 61, Eliot had to suffer another controversy about how she had lived her life. Her widower asked friends to look into the possibility of her being buried in Westminster Abbey (possibly at her suggestion—we can't be sure). Of her contemporaries, Dickens was already buried in Poet's Corner, and Robert Browning, Tennyson, and Hardy would later be too. In his letter of recommendation, the physicist John Tyndall told the Dean of Westminster Arthur Stanley that, if he consented 'to give her shelter, the verdict of the future will be that Dean Stanley has enshrined a woman whose achievements were without parallel in the previous history of womankind'.

Thomas Henry Huxley ('Darwin's bulldog') was characteristically trenchant in his opposition:

> George Eliot is known not only as a great writer, but as a person whose life and opinions were in notorious antagonism to Christian practice in regard to marriage, and Christian theory in regard to dogma . . . One cannot eat one's cake and have it too. Those who elect to be free in thought and deed must not hanker after the rewards, if they are to be so called, which the world offers to those who put up with its fetters.

The petition failed. Eliot was buried close to George Henry Lewes's grave in Highgate cemetery, not far from where Karl Marx would join her a little over two years later. She had asked that Lewes's letters be buried with her. Too controversial for her peers, it would not be long before she was deemed to have not been controversial enough. She survived those controversies too, and a memorial stone was finally laid in her honour in Westminster Abbey in 1980, a century after her death.

Eliot's complicated feminism

George Eliot overcame the disadvantages of life as a young provincial woman through determination and sheer force of intellect, found her way to London where she became the (unofficial) editor of a leading periodical, flouted societal convention and braved ostracism by living with a married man, and went on to become 'the first living novelist' of her time. Yet she has never been a feminist icon.

Feminism made her nervous. She witnessed the stirrings of first-wave feminism in England, and some of the people most vocal in calling for women's rights (members of the 'Langham Place Circle' like Barbara Bodichon and Bessie Rayner Parkes) were her close friends. She demurred, though, when Bodichon sent her a petition on women's rights and refused invitations to write articles on the subject. In 1869, some women could vote in local elections and, a year later, were granted control of their earnings through the Married Women's Property Act, but she remained cautious: 'There is no subject on which I am more inclined to hold my peace and learn, than on the "Women Question". She added, 'I know very little about what is specially good for women—only a few things I feel sure are good for human nature generally' (V.58).

There was, nevertheless, one subject which did animate her: 'the better Education of Women is one of the objects about which I have *no doubt*' (IV.399). She had attended a good local school which had encouraged her to read widely, but left at 16 to run the house for her father after her mother died. A tutor helped her with Italian and German (she had already learnt French), but she would also eventually learn Latin, Greek, Spanish, and Hebrew, mostly under her own steam. There was, of course, no question of attending university. Much later, Eliot would help Emily Davies plan and fund Girton College, Cambridge, founded in 1869.

Eliot's novels unwaveringly attack the personal and social damage caused by the impoverished education of girls. Dorothea is exposed to the 'toy-box history of the world adapted to young ladies'; at Mrs Lemon's school, Rosamond learns 'all that was demanded in the accomplished female—even to extras, such as the getting in and out of a carriage'. The burning shame of being a clever woman dismissed by a patronizing man is seared into her pages. Mr Stelling's judgement that girls have '"a great deal of superficial cleverness; but they couldn't go far into anything"' horrifies Maggie. Bardo tells his daughter Romola that scholarship is not 'reconcileable with the wandering, vagrant propensity of the feminine mind'. The condescension recalls Auguste Comte's assessment that, 'constitutionally in a state of perpetual infancy', women were biologically unsuited to 'concentration'.

If women were infantilized, Eliot insists, society was to blame. Dorothea's 'childlike ideas about marriage' are taught, not innate, and lead her to seek in a partner someone who can belatedly provide her with the education she wasn't given. Eliot conveys the personal despair caused by this lack but, in line with her focus on interdependence, its wider social consequences preoccupy her too. 'We want freedom and culture for woman', Eliot wrote in her essay on Fuller and Wollstonecraft, 'because subjection and ignorance have debased her, and with her, Man'. Men's naive conviction that an uneducated woman will prove easier to manage always backfires: 'so far as obstinacy is concerned, your unreasoning animal is the most unmanageable of creatures'. Eliot's many garrulous women (Lisbeth Bede, Mrs Poyser, Bessy Tulliver, Monna Brigida, Mary Holt) often exhaust their families, bringing to life the 'unmanageable' mind of the uneducated woman.

Eliot did, however, believe in essential differences between the sexes and liked the idea of each sex contributing something distinctive to society. In her essay 'Woman in France', she advocated:

> Let the whole field of reality be laid open to woman as well as to man, and then that which is peculiar in her mental modification, instead of being, as it is now, a source of discord and repulsion between the sexes, will be found to be a necessary complement to the truth and beauty of life.

She outlined what she considered woman's 'special moral influence': 'that exquisite type of gentleness, tenderness, possible maternity suffusing a woman's being with affectionateness' (IV.468). In the novels, women who display masculine traits without counterbalancing womanly virtues are judged harshly. We are made to bristle at Harold Transome's condescension towards his highly capable mother, yet she wishes Harold had died as a child and, 'like all eager-minded women who advance in life without any activity of tenderness or any large sympathy, she had contracted small rigid habits of thinking and acting'.

Although Eliot's female 'saints' Dinah, Romola, and Dorothea are more successfully drawn than her 'priests' Felix and Daniel, the narrator of *Felix Holt* comments that 'The best part of a woman's love is worship', echoing Esther's declaration, '"I am weak—my husband must be greater and nobler than I am."' Esther's hint of playful sarcasm isn't strong enough to offset the fact that the novel has suggested that is indeed the case. The social activist Edith Simcox recorded that Eliot (whom she fell in love with) had told her that 'she had never all her life cared very much for women'. Simcox adds that Eliot 'cared for the womanly ideal, sympathised with women and liked for them to come to her in their troubles', but felt 'far' from them. 'The friendship and intimacy of men was more to her.' It's unsurprising that feminist responses to Eliot have often been frosty.

And so it was that in 1976 Zelda Austen could title an essay 'Why Feminist Critics Are Angry With George Eliot'. In a nutshell, they were angry because her characters fail to do 'what George Eliot did in real life'. Austen quotes a representative reaction: '"It's difficult to avoid feeling some resentment of George Eliot for making her heroines so much less venturesome than she was in her own life."' The same year, a critic had mocked Eliot's 'large-souled' women whose distinction lies not in their deeds but their capacity to 'arouse admiration': Dorothea 'has little of interest to say but a magnificent voice to say it in'. For Kate Millett, writing in 1968, '"Living in Sin"', George Eliot lived the revolution as well, perhaps, but she did not write of it'. As early as 1861, the novelist Dinah Mulock had anticipated such complaints in her review of *The Mill on the Floss*: 'we cannot help asking—what is to become of the hundreds of clever girls, born of uncongenial parents . . .? They must find their way, heaven help them! alone and unaided.' Eliot would surely have responded—did, in effect, respond—that her aim was to represent the typical rather than the exceptional. She was wholly atypical.

Eliot's only attempt to represent a woman who might compare with her in terms of fame is painfully ambivalent. *Daniel Deronda*'s Princess Halm-Eberstein, whose fame as a singer and actress once spread through Europe, has a 'man's force of genius'. She has '"not felt exactly what other women feel—or say they feel"'; she wanted a career rather than children, the thrill of art rather than wifely tenderness, independence rather than family ties. We experience the full force of her cry, '"you can never imagine what it is to have a man's force of genius in you, and yet to suffer the slavery of being a girl"', which we can easily conceive once shook Eliot's own frame. Cold, selfish, and tormented, however, she tries even Deronda's near-boundless powers of sympathy.

The Sibyl

'I shall not readily forget my emotions at seeing George Eliot at the head of the table with her majestic arm carving a leg of mutton', wrote the historian Oscar Browning. Few of those who had once expressed outrage about Eliot could have foreseen that she would become worshipped as a sage. *Middlemarch* completed the transformation. Not only did husbands now bring their wives to dinner, but their daughters begged to be introduced too. One woman was so overawed upon being introduced that she found herself curtsying. People wanted to touch her gown and kiss her feet. Correspondents she had never met consulted her about their domestic problems. Strangers sent gifts. After reading *Middlemarch*, a family thought, '"It would be so nice if we could send Mrs. Lewes" some game.'

The change must have been bewildering. Eliot remained level-headed about what she called in her journal the 'merely egoistic satisfactions of fame', and confessed to a friend that she was occasionally '"tired of being set on a pedestal and expected to vent wisdom"'. But she did want her novels to have an effect. Despite the agonies writing caused her, she persevered from a strong sense that, fiction being her vocation, it was her duty to use it to do good. She gratefully recorded positive responses to *Middlemarch*, having received, her diary notes, 'many deeply affecting assurances of its influence for good on individual minds'. One fan wrote to say Eliot had 'bettered in every way my whole nature'; touched, Eliot thanked her warmly, prompting a deluge of gifts and a correspondence which they started to sign 'mother' and 'daughter'. The 'daughter' was eventually buried beside Eliot in Highgate.

Dickens, punning on the name of the Eliot–Lewes London house where they held a kind of salon, joked about the reverent atmosphere presiding there: 'On Sunday I hope to attend service at the Priory.' Charles Godfrey Leland reported that there was an impression in America that 'something enormous, marvellous, and inspired went on at these receptions, and that George Eliot posed as a Pythia or Sibyl, as the great leading mind of England, and lectured while we listened'. The image of a Sibyl stuck and was used alike by Eliot's denigrators and worshippers. The ever-waspish Eliza Lynn Linton was among the former, sneering that Eliot 'was always the goddess on her pedestal . . .—never did she throw aside the trappings or the airs of the benign Sibyl.'

The writer F. H. Myers, firmly in the category of the worshippers, famously described a walk they shared at Trinity College, Cambridge, on a rainy May evening when Eliot,

> stirred somewhat beyond her wont, and taking as her text the three words which have been used so often as the inspiring trumpet-calls of men,—the words *God, Immortality, Duty,*—pronounced, with terrible earnestness, how inconceivable was the *first*, how unbelievable the *second*, and yet how peremptory and absolute the *third*.

The 'strenuous seriousness' Myers so admired lent her no favours with the iconoclastic *fin-de-siècle* and early 20th-century writers already predisposed to overthrow their parents' values. Edmund Gosse produced a snobbish, Lytton-Stracheyesque portrait of Lewes and Eliot going home in a carriage, one

> a large, thickset sybil, dreamy and immobile, whose massive features, somewhat grim when seen in profile, were incongruously bordered by a hat, always in the height of the Paris fashion, which in those days commonly included an immense ostrich feather; this was George Eliot. The contrast between the solemnity of the face and the frivolity of the headgear had something pathetic and provincial about it.

Eliot's sage-like reputation was not, or not entirely, of her own doing: it was cemented by two men. The first was 'the Gusher', the nickname John Blackwood gave to Alexander Main. This super-fan began corresponding with Eliot in 1871 and received permission to publish a book called *Wise, Witty, and Tender Sayings in Prose and Verse, Selected from the Works of George Eliot*. What Shakespeare did for drama, Main asserts, George Eliot has done for the novel, which she has 'for ever sanctified' by 'making it the vehicle of the grandest and most uncompromising moral truth'. The work is organized by novel (with additional chapters on the poems) and selects quotations categorized into sayings by 'George Eliot (*in propria persona*)' (thereby collapsing the distinction between author and narrator) and by her characters. He chose such gems as 'The delicate-tendrilled plant must have something to cling to' and 'Sleep comes to the perplexed—if the perplexed are only weary enough'.

Hungry for more, Main also published *The George Eliot Birthday Book* (1878), which gives an Eliot quotation or two for each day of the year with, on the facing page, a blank space on which to write the birthdays of friends and family (Figure 9). Eliot assisted Main with his labours but expressed misgivings: the very concept of extracts undermined 'the ends I seek by my works as wholes', she grumbled to her publisher; they did violence to the aesthetic integrity of her work and made them seem dangerously close to the maxims she had so repeatedly cautioned against. To separate her work into '"direct"' and '"indirect"' teaching (V.459) was to overlook the ways in which form and style, rather than mere matter, articulated her thought.

John Walter Cross made matters worse. Shortly after his wife's death, Cross sifted through her papers to compile *George Eliot's Life as Related in her Letters and Journals*. The biography accomplished at least three things. It unveiled further autobiographical parallels in the novels. It revealed the complex intellectual influences that had informed the fiction from the very

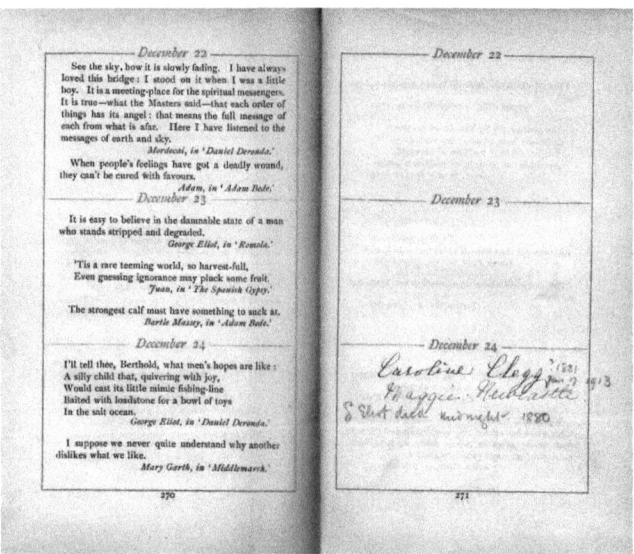

December 22

See the sky, how it is slowly fading. I have always loved this bridge : I stood on it when I was a little boy. It is a meeting-place for the spiritual messengers. It is true—what the Masters said—that each order of things has its angel : that means the full message of each from what is afar. Here I have listened to the messages of earth and sky.

Mordecai, in 'Daniel Deronda.'

When people's feelings have got a deadly wound, they can't be cured with favours.

Adam, in 'Adam Bede.'

December 23

It is easy to believe in the damnable state of a man who stands stripped and degraded.

George Eliot, in 'Romola.'

'Tis a rare teeming world, so harvest-full,
Even guessing ignorance may pluck some fruit.

Juan, in 'The Spanish Gipsy.'

The strongest calf must have something to suck at.

Bartle Massey, in 'Adam Bede.'

December 24

I'll tell thee, Berthold, what men's hopes are like :
A silly child that, quivering with joy,
Would cast its little mimic fishing-line
Baited with loadstone for a bowl of toys
In the salt ocean.

George Eliot, in 'Daniel Deronda.'

I suppose we never quite understand why another dislikes what we like.

Mary Garth, in 'Middlemarch.'

270

December 22

December 23

December 24

Caroline Clegg
Maggie Hubbard
G Eliot died midnight 1880

271

9. One result of Alexander Main's increasingly embarrassing adulation was *The George Eliot Birthday Book*. Eliot worried that such books might be 'the vulgarest thing in the book stalls' (VI.423). The owner of this copy dutifully entered Eliot's death, misdating it by two days.

start, disabusing many readers of the supposition that it was only later in her career that, moving away from more bucolic settings, her agnosticism grew. ('Is this the woman who wrote *Adam Bede*?', marvelled Margaret Oliphant in her review of it.) Finally, if Main fabricated a sententious Eliot, Cross packaged a dour one. Eliot once more became the victim of over-zealous editing: on high alert for any details that might injure her reputation, Cross's interventions included swapping references Eliot made to her toes to the more demure fingers. The work has since become a byword for bad Victorian biography and silly Victorian prudery—Gladstone memorably quipped that 'It is not a Life at all. It is a Reticence in three volumes.'

Such interference naturally did more harm than good in the eyes of a generation more likely to worship at the altar of what the critic George Saintsbury called 'the great god Nonsense'. Oliphant, already given to envy, saw confirmation that Eliot 'was always on duty, never relaxing, her letters ponderous beyond description'. The judgement of Henry James's sister Alice was more devastating still: 'What a lifeless, diseased, self-conscious being she must have been! Not one burst of joy, not one ray of humour, not one living breath in one of her letters or journals.' She gave off a sense of 'mildew'. The fellow apostate William Hale White, who knew what Eliot had been, lamented that Cross had 'made her too "respectable"'. She had been removed from the class 'of the Insurgents, to one more genteel, but certainly not so interesting'.

Eliot's artistic reputation has since recovered, but the damage done to the comic George Eliot has been permanent. Reading her first drafts, Lewes immediately decreed her '"pathos"' better than her '"fun"', and few have disagreed. Her satire could be dynamic (witness 'Silly Novels by Lady Novelists')—indeed, her first reviewers worried that she might be too satirical and was following too closely in Thackeray's path. She had a keen eye for the ludicrous, such as Mrs Pullet performing intense grief while taking great care to protect her fashionable clothes from harm. She could be mischievous ('Ineffable moment! when the man you secretly hate sends you a Latin epigram with a false gender', the narrator jokes in *Romola*). Her ear for the comic energy of speech was sharp; the way she captures Mr Brooke's meandering vagueness is hard to fault:

'I remember when we were all reading Adam Smith. *There* is a book, now. I took in all the new ideas at one time—human perfectibility, now. But some say, history moves in circles; and that may be very well argued; I have argued it myself. The fact is, human reason may carry you a little too far—over the hedge, in fact. It carried me a good way at one time; but I saw it would not do. I pulled up; I pulled up in time. But not too hard.'

But even her comedy was enlisted in the overarching ambition of stimulating greater fellow-feeling, and it's the seriousness of the project rather than the humour of the treatment for which she is best known.

—but why always *Middlemarch*?

No project has felt more serious than *Middlemarch*. It wasn't always *Middlemarch*. Eliot thought *Romola* superior; her readers usually preferred *Adam Bede*. Its first reviewers recognized a monumental achievement—for one, 'it bids more than fair to be one of the great books of the world' and, for another, 'to the mind of the day there is scarcely anything so rousing in all literature'— but a new generation eager to distance itself from its elders was already sharpening its knives. Samuel Butler began writing *The Way of All Flesh* the same year he read *Middlemarch*, which he judged 'a long-winded piece of studied brag'. Edmund Gosse, author of his own memoir on the misery of growing up Victorian, *Father and Son*, found it a 'remarkable instance of elaborate mental resources misapplied'. These and subsequent attacks were so effective that the historian Asa Briggs could state that 'Eliot was only in the process of being rediscovered and reassessed in 1948'.

'Another "great books" poll boringly confirms the dominance of *Middlemarch*', a weary headline read in reaction to a 2015 BBC Culture survey of 82 international (but not UK-based) literary critics on 'the greatest British novels'. A measure of *Middlemarch's* astonishing cultural elevation in the last few decades is that its supremacy is perceived as a cliché rather than a recent development. Certainly, British novelists have discussed this domination—*Middlemarch* not necessarily as their 'favourite' novel but the 'best'—like a fait accompli. For Martin Amis, 'I don't think there is much argument about *Middlemarch* being the novel of the 19th century. I would say that it is the central English novel.' Julian Barnes called it 'the greatest British novel of the 19th century, and probably of any century', and A. S. Byatt deemed it 'possible to argue that *Middlemarch* is the greatest English novel'.

The sanctification of *Middlemarch* is all the more intriguing because Eliot is rarely touted as the greatest 19th-century novelist, the crown for which commonly goes to Austen or Dickens. Nonetheless, as a single novel, *Middlemarch* reigns supreme as a cultural marker. 'The roar on the other side of silence', or sometimes simply 'the other side of silence', has been used as the title of over a dozen books including thrillers, Christian meditation guides, self-help autobiographies, and oral histories. It features in the U2 song 'Breathe'. How did the work's fortunes change so dramatically?

Readers had outgrown the modernists' grudge, for one. But another answer deals with changing attitudes to literary form. Henry James famously declared of *Middlemarch* that 'It sets a limit, we think, to the development of the old-fashioned English novel'. It made the Victorian writer Robert Laing 'ponder whether the course of the English novel may not be well-nigh run'. Neither meant it as a compliment. But as Eliot wrote in the novel, 'Every limit is a beginning as well as an ending'. For later readers, it teeters intriguingly on a literary knife-edge: it is both the ultimate encapsulation of Victorian High Realism (with its intrusive omniscient narrator, panoramic vision, moral earnestness) and an extraordinarily self-aware rendition of that mode (with reflections on the limitations of realism and sympathy, microscopic psychological dissections, and sustained irony). For Victorian readers looking forward, there was surely nowhere else for the novel to go. For modern critics looking backward, it anticipated 20th-century concerns.

Eliot was ahead of the curve in underscoring the organic nature of her novels at a time when Victorian reviewers had different priorities, while modernists' recoil from literature seeking to teach made them assume that the plots were there, Mary Poppins-style, simply to help the medicine go down. In the 1950s, as Victorian studies in general were developing in English departments, Barbara Hardy helped bring out Eliot's artful handling of imagistic patterns and motifs. In 1892, Rabindranath Tagore had compared her work to a jackfruit, 'not only huge in size and heavy in weight but also difficult to tolerate for the puny digestive system of a single human being'. The sheer heft of Eliot's novels had distracted readers from the astonishing precision and control of her shortest clauses. As Howard Jacobson put it for the BBC in 2017, Eliot wrote *Middlemarch*

> not with the remoteness of the cleric who's been sermonising to a dozing congregation for half a century, but as a novelist, for whom thought is not to be separated from the senses; whose language is tactile, not abstract; whose words pulse with the blood of life, as though they are characters in the drama themselves.

Her complexity has also been redeemed on psychological grounds. Virginia Woolf's well-known statement in 1919 that *Middlemarch* 'is one of the few English novels written for grown-up people' put her at odds with her contemporaries. We can't be sure what she had in mind, but it's certainly a novel if not for middle-aged readers then at least about mid-life disillusion. Margaret Atwood, having taught the novel, summarized her experience:

> The 18-year olds said, 'We hate this book because the characters marry the wrong people, they make mistakes, they have failures, and we're never going to do that.' And the grown-ups said, 'We love this book because the people marry the wrong people, they make mistakes, they have failures, and that's what life is about.'

Soon after *Middlemarch* appeared, Walter Pater gave his famous definition of 'success in life': 'To burn always with this hard, gemlike flame, to maintain this ecstasy'. This feels like an adolescent sentiment that Eliot implicitly rebuts in *Daniel Deronda*, where she calmly notes that 'a great deal of life goes on without strong passion': shoelaces need to be tied, bills have to be paid.

Woolf was echoed in another landmark study: F. R. Leavis's 1948 work *The Great Tradition* states that, to deserve the title of 'great English novelist', a writer's corpus must be 'addressed to the adult mind'. Eliot passes Leavis's test. She is one of five writers—with Austen, James, Conrad, and Lawrence—'distinguished by a vital capacity for experience, a kind of reverent openness before life, and a marked moral intensity'. Leavis led the way in championing Eliot's later novels rather than the early works that had until then been largely preferred; their charm is precisely, for him, what makes them slighter achievements. The later are all the better for seeming less Victorian.

Leavis recast as positive qualities what had before been lamented as showy. Henry James found Eliot's prose 'too clever by half. The author wishes to say too many things, and to say them too well.' Leslie Stephen had attempted a Leavis-like defence immediately after her death: 'She is convicted upon conclusive evidence of having indulged in ideas . . . I confess that, for my part, I am rather glad to find ideas anywhere. They are not very common'. But the moment was unpropitious, and the second half of the 20th century proved more receptive to the notion that 'luminous intelligence' (Leavis's words) might not prove a drawback for a novelist. Writing so soon after the devastation of the Second World War, Eliot's unswerving, demanding humanism might also have felt vital. It may do so still.

The way we read *Middlemarch* now isn't, in fact, so different from what her first readers were affected by beyond anything about the work. No one, they agreed, had ever written characters like this. For critics writing in the first decade after the novel's appearance, it marked 'an epoch in the history of fiction in so far as its incidents are taken from the inner life, as the action is developed by the direct influence of mind on mind and character on character'; 'never before have so keen and varied an observation, so deep an insight into character and motives' come together. Dorothea's dawning realization of Casaubon's inadequacies is 'just such a one as only George Eliot could either conceive or execute'; 'no one studies more carefully the relations between the characters of parents and their children'; Rosamond is the 'finest picture of that shallowness which constitutes absolute incapacity for either deep feeling or true morality, we have ever met with in English literature'.

Balzac is meant to have called out, as he lay dying, for the doctor he had invented; Thackeray visited the buildings in Belgium where Becky Sharp lived; Dickens claimed that his characters insisted on developing their stories as they, rather than he, saw fit. Eliot had her own stories, her husband shared, about how, when writing, 'there was a "not herself" which took possession of her, and that she felt her own personality to be merely the instrument through which this spirit, as it were, was acting'. Critics react to accounts of this nature with scepticism. Theoretical approaches to the Victorian novel have instead stressed the coercive control authors exert over their characters. For the critic D. A. Miller, notoriously, interjections like 'poor Lydgate' and 'poor Rosamond' are disingenuous expressions occluding the fact that the narrator (the 'master-voice') holds all the cards: it's the 'basic move of a familiar power play'.

Yet it's the bewildering sense of her characters' autonomy that has struck many readers of *Middlemarch*. One Victorian reviewer wanted to understand where his impulse to take sides with characters against Eliot came from. Inclined at first to see her bias against Rosamond as a blemish, he then saw it as an impressive instance of the novelist permitting characters to exist in themselves:

> Her characters are so real that they have a life and body of their own quite distinct from her criticisms on them; and one is

conscious at times of taking part with her characters against the author, and accusing her of availing herself unfairly of the privilege of author, by adding a trait that bears out her own *criticism* rather than her own imaginative conception.

A response written nearly 150 years later similarly celebrates the manner in which Eliot 'discovers' her characters' motivations: '"Discovers"' because Eliot, perhaps more than any other English novelist, seems to approach those characters as beings who already exist'.

Philosophers like Fredric Jameson have become increasingly attuned to the ways in which Eliot's fiction strikingly anticipates many aspects of existentialism—in her depiction of characters' self-deception (or 'bad faith') and their embattled relationship with social convention, the emphasis on choice and responsibility, and her acknowledgement of each character's centre of self. Maggie, though, rather than Dorothea, is who a young Simone de Beauvoir identified with:

> Maggie Tulliver, like myself, was torn between others and herself: I recognized myself in her. She too was dark, loved nature and books and life, was too headstrong to be able to observe the conventions of her respectable surroundings.

Although she found her way to an early 20th-century French teenager, Eliot has not always found a warm reception beyond Britain. In the 1898 Bengali novel *Kahake* by Swarnakumari Devi, a passionate Eliot fan describes how, reading her work, he is 'happy in drowning my individuality in the great sea of existence', but his interlocutor is unconvinced. In the 1992 novel *In the Eye of the Sun* by the Egyptian novelist Ahdaf Soueif, characters again fall out over Eliot's merits: '"I think Asya was saying she was a great writer and he was saying she wasn't."' In the 2017 novel *Pachinko* by the Korean-American novelist Min Jin Lee, university students in Tokyo are divided between those who believe that '"Everything by George Eliot is perfect"' and those who find her a '"bore"'.

Middlemarch has not turned into the pinnacle of Eliot's achievement in all countries. In some cases, debates about her status grew out of an imperialist legacy. The colonial spread of the Cambridge Local Examination from 1864 introduced students around the globe to a range of 19th-century British novelists like Walter Scott, but Eliot's fiction first appeared as a set text only in 1919, and it was as the author of *Silas Marner* that she was principally known. (*Middlemarch* did, however, appear as early as 1891 on the MA syllabus of the University of Calcutta.) Postcolonial criticism has also shaped recent arguments that the supposed greatness of 'great British novels', meaning predominantly 19th-century novels, was promoted by the structuralist reading strategies of the 1970s–1980s rather than forming an enduring, universal truth. Dethroning realism as the 'ur-form of the novel'—as the form against which other novels are measured—would, these accounts stress, have implications for attitudes towards non-Western novels.

Such assumptions about the legacy of the Victorian novel may stand behind the tendency to describe, or even self-label, other novels as a country's equivalent to *Middlemarch*: Soueif's novel (whose epitaph is the 'roar on the other side of silence') has been called an 'Egyptian Middlemarch', for example, and Vikram Seth's 1993 novel *A Suitable Boy* was advertised as an 'Indian Middlemarch'. The Sri Lankan novelist Shyam Selvadurai invites a similar comparison in his 1998 work *Cinnamon Gardens* by choosing as his epigraph the conclusion of *Middlemarch*. Mostly, though, *Middlemarch* appears to have been politely ignored beyond its main Anglo-American readership. It was almost immediately translated into Danish, Dutch, German, Norwegian, and Hungarian, but not into Japanese until 1975, Spanish until 1984, or Chinese until 1987.

In 1861 the Norwegian linguist Ivar Aasen translated excerpts of *Adam Bede* as part of a project to promote Norwegian regional dialects in opposition to the Danish-influenced official language. *The Spanish Gypsy* held special resonance for 19th-century African-American writers. The 'Jewish question' agitating *fin-de-siècle* Russia gave *Daniel Deronda* unusual prominence there. *Silas Marner*, which culminates with Eppie refusing a life of wealth to remain with Silas, has been popular in 20th-century communist regimes—although readers have regretted that Eliot didn't go far enough in advocating outright revolution. 'So fast does a little leaven spread within us—so incalculable is the effect of one personality on another', Eliot writes in *Felix Holt*. Literary reception is similarly unpredictable.

Epilogue

At the end of 1857 George Eliot felt overcome with gratitude. She often took stock of a closing year in her journal, and on 19 December she was full of 'thankful solemn thoughts—feeling the great and unhoped for blessings that have been given me in life'. Her first short stories had been published and would soon appear as a book, and two months earlier she had begun her first novel. On a beautiful, Spring-like Christmas day, she ate her festive turkey with George Henry Lewes in a 'happy "solitude à deux"'; they had been together now for over four years.

This contentment stayed with her on New Year's Eve, when she acknowledged the joy that a 'greater capacity for moral and intellectual enjoyment' and 'the blessedness of a perfect love and union' had recently brought her. She added: 'Few women, I fear have had such reason as I have to think the long sad years of youth were worth living for the sake of middle age.'

Eliot thought of herself as someone who had been given the chance to start life again in her mid-thirties. Her 24-year career as a novelist would ultimately be substantially shorter than the 37 years she spent preparing for it, during many of which she believed herself destined for a life of solitude and obscurity. When her husband John Walter Cross later asked if she wanted to write her autobiography, she replied: '"The only thing I should care much to dwell on would be the absolute despair I suffered from of ever being able to achieve anything. No one could ever have felt greater despair."' The melancholy 'Finale' of *Middlemarch* might have been hers.

Although five of her seven novels are set in the Midlands, as well as most of her short fiction, 'George Eliot' never set foot there. Marian Evans's last visit to the Warwickshire towns and countryside that feed so much of her work appears to have been in December 1855, when she spent Christmas with her sister nine months before starting 'The Sad Fortunes of the Reverend Amos Barton'. (Her family would know nothing about Lewes until May 1857.) In *Middlemarch*, she notes:

> In watching effects, if only of an electric battery, it is often necessary to change our place and examine a particular mixture or group at some distance from the point where the movement we are interested in was set up.

She was set up in Warwickshire; she examined from London. The Midlands affected not just where her novels are set, but what they're about and how they're written, but from the day she began writing them it lived only in her memory, her imagination, and through the letters she exchanged.

Dickens wrote and lived in London. Gaskell penned her industrial novels from Manchester. The Brontës, like their novels, seem inextricable from the moors that surrounded them. Hardy built his own house in Dorchester with the proceeds of his Dorset novels. And yet it is Eliot, to whom the label of 'realist' has been most persistently attached, and with it the notion of close observation and a 'faithful' representation of the world, who wrote from afar. 'Faithful' can mean accuracy, of course, but it can also mean loyalty, duty, and a belief that can, but needn't, be religious. It is a word that speaks of attachments as well as studiousness, of the eye as well as the heart. These might not always be entirely compatible.

The contrasts in Eliot's life and work can feel startling. They sometimes felt startling to Eliot. Her contemporaries were quick to pick up on what they saw as a growing discrepancy between the novels' provincial concerns and their cosmopolitan style. Readers have often felt the pull of competing elements in her novels and have instinctively set about separating them: Gwendolen but not Daniel; the entertaining, sarcastic narrator but not the dour, moralizing one; the early, charming novels but not the late, demanding ones; the Midlands but not Italy.

Eliot resisted such partitions. She would surely have approved *The Times*'s tribute after her death: 'She blended the intellectual, the philosophical, and the metaphysical with all that was most simple, most natural and most human.' 'Blend' was always a favourite word; 'mixture' became one. Like the body and the mind, George Eliot and Marian Evans held parallel but not separate lives, and she never ceased moving flexibly, unpredictably, and often poignantly, between the two.

References

Prologue

Gillian Beer, 'What's Not in *Middlemarch*', in *Middlemarch in the Twenty-First Century*, ed. Karen Chase (Oxford, 2006), 15–35.

David Carroll, 'Introduction', in *George Eliot: The Critical Heritage*, ed. David Carroll (London, 2000), 6.

Thackeray to Mrs Carmichael-Smyth (1848), *The Letters and Private Papers of William Makepeace Thackeray, Vol. II*, ed. Gordon N. Ray (Cambridge, Mass., 1946), 383.

John Henry Newman (1858 lecture), *The Idea of a University*, ed. Martin J. Svaglic (Notre Dame, Ind., 1982), 208.

Oliver Goldsmith, *Retaliation: A Poem* (London, 1774), 8.

Henry James, 'Preface', *The Novels and Tales of Henry James. Vol. VII: The Tragic Muse* (New York, 1907), x.

Nathan Heller, 'The End of the English Major', *The New Yorker* (27 February 2023), 30.

[Unsigned], 'George Eliot's Life', *The Times* (27 January 1885), 4.

Lewes Journal, in Gordon S. Haight, *George Eliot: A Biography* (1968; repr. London, 1985), 273.

[E. S. Dallas] (1859), *Critical Heritage*, 77.

Charles Buxton to the Earl of Malmesbury, House of Commons (8 March 1859), *Hansard*, 1508.

R. E. Francillon (1876); William Barry (1881), *Critical Heritage*, 396, 38.

Chapter 1: Gossip

Robert Evans Journal (1842), in Haight, *George Eliot*, 40.

Eliot, cited in Haight, *George Eliot*, 19.

Eliot, reported in Emily Davies to Jane Crow (1868), in *Emily Davies: Collected Letters 1861–1875*, ed. Ann B. Murphy and Deirdre Baftery (Charlottesville, Va, 2004), 287.

K. K. Collins (ed.), *George Eliot: Interviews and Recollections* (Basingstoke, 2010), 79, 81.

Lewes to Charlotte Brontë, *The Letters of Charlotte Brontë*, ed. Margaret Smith (Oxford, 1995–2004), II, 416 n. 5.

Charles Bray (1885) and George Combe (1854), in Haight, *George Eliot*, 51, 166.

John Walter Cross, *George Eliot's Life as Related in Her Letters and Journals* (Edinburgh, 1885), I, 431.

Eliot, 'Woman in France' (1854), in *Essays*, 54.

[Unsigned], *Saturday Review* (1860), *Critical Heritage*, 114, 118.

Robert Southey to Charlotte Brontë (1837), *Letters of Charlotte Brontë*, I, 165–7.

Gaskell to Eliot (1859), *The Letters of Mrs Gaskell*, ed. J. A. V. Chapple and Arthur Pollard (Manchester, 1966), 592.

Henry Crabb Robinson (1859), *Critical Heritage*, 12.

Athenaeum, in Haight, *George Eliot*, III.109 n. 1.

Eliot (1859), *Journals*, 78.

On gossip and for a rich exploration of how Eliot's life informed her works, see Rosemarie Bodenheimer, *The Real Life of Mary Ann Evans* (Ithaca, NY, 1994).

A. V. Dicey (1873), *Critical Heritage*, 340.

Margaret Oliphant, *The Autobiography of Mrs. Oliphant* (1899), ed. Mrs Harry Coghill (Chicago, 1988), 5.

Edith Simcox, *Autobiography of a Shirtmaker*, ed. Constance M. Fulmer and Margaret E. Barfield (New York, 1998), 117.

Henry James (1885), *Critical Heritage*, 39.

Virginia Woolf, 'George Eliot', *TLS* (20 November 1919), 658.

Eliot, *Middlemarch*, ed. David Carroll (Oxford, 1992), 825 n.1.

[Unsigned], *Canadian Monthly* (1873), *Critical Heritage*, 29.

Chapter 2: Realism

John Ruskin, *Modern Painters: Of Mountain Beauty* (London, 1856), 60.

Eliot, 'The Natural History of German Life' (1856), *Essays*, 268–71.

Eliot, 'Art and Belles Lettres [Ruskin]', *Westminster Review*, 45 (1856), 343.

[Unsigned], *Dublin University Magazine* (1861), *Critical Heritage*, 148.

[Lewes], 'Realism in Art', *Westminster Review*, 70 (1858), 493.

Eliot, 'Worldliness and Other-Worldliness' (1857), *Essays*, 367.

[Unsigned], *Dublin University Magazine* (1862), *Critical Heritage*, 194.

Eliot, 'Silly Novels by Lady Novelists' (1856), *Essays*, 302, 309.

Eliot, 'Belles Lettres [*Constance Herbert*]' (1855), *Essays*, 134–5.

Eliot, 'The Morality of Wilhelm Meister' (1855), *Essays*, 145.

Eliot, 'The Natural History of German Life', 268, 271.

[W. Lucas Collins] (1859), *Critical Heritage*, 10.

Kathryn Hughes, *Victorians Undone* (London, 2017), 157.

William Wordsworth to Charles James Fox (1801), in *The Letters of William and Dorothy Wordsworth*, ed. Ernest de Selincourt and Chester L. Shaver (Oxford, 1967–93), I, 314–15.

William Wordsworth, *The Prelude* (1805), Book XII, lines 145–68.

[E. S. Dallas] (1859); *Spectator* (1860); *Saturday Review* (1861); *Examiner* (1859); *Saturday Review* (1859); *London Quarterly Review* (1860); [E. S. Dallas] (1860); John Ruskin (n.d.); *Dublin University Magazine* (1862); Swinburne (1877); R. H. Hutton (1866); Henry James (1873); Robert Louis Stevenson (1911); all in *Critical Heritage*, 79–80, 109, 171, 11, 76, 249, 132, 167, 190, 163, 259, 356, 33.

Leslie Stephen, *George Eliot* (London, 1902), 104.

Eliot, 'Worldliness and Other-Worldliness', 382.

Gustave Flaubert to Louise Colet (1852), *The Letters of Gustave Flaubert, 1830–1857*, ed. Francis Steegmuller (Cambridge, Mass., 1980), 154.

George Gissing, *New Grub Street* (1891), ed. Katherine Mullin (Oxford, 2016), 128.

Eliot, 'The Antigone and its Moral' (1856), *Essays*, 263–4.

E. S. Dallas, *The Gay Science* (London, 1866), II, 296–7.

Henry James (1873), *Critical Heritage*, 357.

Chapter 3: Sympathy

W. H. Mallock, (1879), *Critical Heritage*, 453.

Feuerbach, *The Essence of Christianity* (1854), 14, 2, 271.

[E. S. Dallas] (1859), *Critical Heritage*, 78.

Friedrich Nietzsche, *Twilight of the Idols* (1889), trans. Duncan Large (Oxford, 1998), 45.

G. M. Young, 'The Greatest Victorian', *Victorian Essays*, ed.
    W. D. Handcock (London, 1962), 124.

[A. V. Dicey] (1873); G. P. Lathrop (1874), *Critical Heritage*, 348, 24.

George Acorn, *One of the Multitude* (London, 1911), 49.

[Unsigned], *Dublin University Magazine* (1861), *Critical
    Heritage*, 152.

Eliot, 'The Morality of Wilhelm Meister', 146.

Eliot, 'Recollections of Ilfracombe' (1856), *Journals*, 264–5.

Feuerbach, *The Essence of Christianity*, 30.

Gillian Beer, *George Eliot* (Brighton, 1986), 113.

Eliot, 'The Progress of the Intellect' (1851), *Essays*, 31.

Feuerbach, *The Essence of Christianity*, 157.

Eliot (1869), *Journals*, 134, 141.

A. V. Dicey (1873), *Critical Heritage*, 348.

Eliot, 'Notes on Form in Art' (1868), *Essays*, 433.

[R. H. Hutton] (1872), *Critical Heritage*, 306.

Elizabeth Malleson; Sidney Colvin, both in *Interviews and
    Recollections*, 69, 91.

Feuerbach, *The Essence of Christianity*, 82, 53.

Chapter 4: Cognition

D. H. Lawrence, cited in *D. H. Lawrence: A Personal Record by
    E.T. (Jessie Chambers)* (London, 1935), 105.

Samuel Taylor Coleridge (1810), *Collected Letters of Samuel Taylor
    Coleridge*, ed. Earl Leslie Griggs (Oxford, 1956–71), III, 282.

Sigmund Freud to Martha Bernays (1882), in Ernest Jones, *Sigmund
    Freud: Life and Work* (New York, 1953–7), I, 191.

Eliot, 'The Progress of the Intellect', 31.

On Victorian reviewing and consistency of character, see Carroll, *The
    Critical Heritage*, 2.

[Unsigned], '*Middlemarch:* Second Notice', *Saturday Review* (21
    December 1872), 796.

Eliot, 'The Natural History of German Life', 267.

David Carroll, *George Eliot and the Conflict of Interpretations*
    (Cambridge, 2009), 146.

John Chapman, 'Adam Bede', *Westminster Review*, 71 (April
    1859), 510.

Leslie Stephen (1881), *Critical Heritage*, 475.

Matthew Arnold, *Culture and Anarchy* (1869), ed. Jane Garnett
    (Oxford, 2006), 107, 111.

Samuel Johnson, *Rasselas* (1759), ed. Thomas Keymer (Oxford, 2009), 19.

Eliot, 'Worldliness and Other-Worldliness', 370.

Two books explore Eliot's self-checking impulse particularly well: Rosemarie Bodenheimer, *The Real Life of Mary Ann Evans*, especially chapter 3, and Philip Davis, *The Transferred Life of George Eliot* (Oxford, 2017).

Spinoza, *Ethics*, 138–9, 133, 129.

Clare Carlisle, 'George Eliot's Spinoza: An Introduction', Spinoza, *Ethics*, 42.

Mathilde Blind, *George Eliot* (London, 1883), 164.

George Henry Lewes, *The Physiology of Common Life* (London, 1859), I, 63, 66.

John Keats to J. H. Reynolds (1818), in *Selected Letters*, ed. Robert Gittings (Oxford, 2002), 88. See Jill L. Matus, 'George Eliot', in *The Cambridge Companion to English Novelists*, ed. Adrian Poole (Cambridge, 2009), 225–41, for a brief but insightful overview of Eliot and Victorian physiology.

Chapter 5: Meliorism

Sidney Colvin (1873); R. H. Hutton, *Critical Heritage*, 332, 176.

J. A. Froude, *Thomas Carlyle: A History of His Life in London 1834–1881* (London, 1884), I, 290–1.

Eliot (1869), *Journals*, 138; (1877), *Journals*, 148.

Wordsworth, *The Prelude*, XII, 269–70.

Eliot, 'Address to Working Men, by Felix Holt', *Blackwood's Magazine* (January 1868), 5.

Eliot, 'The Natural History of German Life', 287.

Eliot, 'Margaret Fuller and Mary Wollstonecraft' (1855), *Essays*, 205.

Henry James, *English Hours* (Boston, 1905), 197.

Thomas Carlyle, *Heroes, Hero-Worship and the Heroic in History* (London, 1841), 362.

Thomas Babington Macaulay, 'History' (1828), *The Miscellaneous Writings of Lord Macaulay* (London, 1865), 127.

John Richard Green, *A Short History of the English People* (London, 1874), vi.

Homer, *The Odyssey*, trans. Emily Wilson (New York, 2017), VIII, 522–8.

Gerard Manley Hopkins, 'Notes on Contemplation' (1881), *The Sermons and Devotional Writings of Gerard Manley Hopkins*, ed. Christopher Devin (London, 1959), 176.

Chapter 6: Afterlife

John Tyndall to Arthur Stanley (1880); Thomas Henry Huxley (1880), in Haight, *George Eliot*, 548–9.

Auguste Comte, *The Positive Philosophy*, trans. Harriet Martineau (London, 1853), II, 135.

Eliot, 'Margaret Fuller and Mary Wollstonecraft', 205.

Edith Simcox, *Autobiography of a Shirtmaker*, 117.

Zelda Austen, 'Why Feminist Critics Are Angry With George Eliot', *College English*, 37 (February 1976), 549.

Ellen Moers, *Literary Women* (New York, 1976), 195.

Zelda Austen, 'Why Feminist Critics Are Angry With George Eliot', 550.

Kate Millett, *Sexual Politics* (New York, 1970), 139.

Dinah Mulock (1861), *Critical Heritage*, 157.

Oscar Browning, in *Interviews and Recollections*, 188.

Reported by Benjamin Jowett (1872), in Haight, *George Eliot*, 451.

Eliot (1873), *Journals*, 143.

Eliot, reported by Georgiana-Burne Jones, in *Interviews and Recollections*, 215.

Elma Stuart to Eliot (1872), in Haight, *George Eliot*, 451–2.

Charles Dickens to Eliot (1870), in *The Letters of Charles Dickens: 1858–1870*, ed. Walter Dexter (London, 1938), 767.

Charles Godfrey Leland; Eliza Lynn Linton; F. H. Myers; Edmund Gosse, all in *Interviews and Recollections*, 101, 116, 155, 126.

Alexander Main, *Wise, Witty, and Tender Sayings in Prose and Verse, Selected from the Works of George Eliot* (Edinburgh, 1871), ix–x.

Margaret Oliphant (1885), in *Critical Heritage*, 40.

William Gladstone, in E. F. Benson, *As We Were: A Victorian Peep-Show* (London, 1930), 111.

George Saintsbury (1891), in *Critical Heritage*, 42.

Margaret Oliphant, *Autobiography*, 7.

Alice James (1889), *Diary*, ed. Leon Edel (New York, 1934), 41.

William Hale White, in *Interviews and Recollections*, 36.

Lewes to Eliot, in Eliot, 'How I Came to Write Fiction', *Journals*, 290.

[R. H. Hutton] (1872); Sidney Colvin (1873), in *Critical Heritage*, 302, 331.

Samuel Butler (1873), *Letters between Samuel Butler and Miss E. M. A. Savage (1871-1885)*, ed. Geoffrey Keynes and Brian Hill (London, 1935), 40.

Edmund Gosse (1919), in *Aspects and Impressions* (London, 1922), 14.

Asa Briggs, in *The Collected Essays of Asa Briggs* (Urbana, IL., 1985), II, 49.

Laura Marsh, 'Another "great books" poll boringly confirms the dominance of *Middlemarch*', *The New Republic* (7 December 2015).

Martin Amis, in 'What *Middlemarch* means to me', *Guardian* (28 February 2014).

Julian Barnes, in Shusha Guppy, 'The Art of Fiction no. 165', *Paris Review* (Winter 2000).

A. S. Byatt, 'Wit and Wisdom', *Guardian* (4 August 2007).

Henry James (1873), in *Critical Heritage*, 359.

Robert Laing, 'Middlemarch', *Quarterly Review* (April 1873), 359.

Barbara Hardy, *The Novels of George Eliot* (London, 1959).

Rabindranath Tagore (1947), in Abhishek Sarkar and Ballari Das, 'Of Literary Jackfruits and the Female Sage: The Colonial Bengali Reception of George Eliot', *Literature Compass* (October 2020), 4.

Howard Jacobson, 'A Point of View: Renouncing *Middlemarch*', *BBC Radio 4* (4 June 2017), transcription mine.

Virginia Woolf, 'George Eliot', 658.

Margaret Atwood, in Samantha Leach, Margaret Atwood Q&A, *Bustle* (20 November 2020).

Walter Pater, *Studies in the History of the Renaissance* (1873), ed. Matthew Beaumont (Oxford, 2010), 188.

F. R. Leavis, *The Great Tradition* (London, 1948), 172, 9, 123.

Henry James (1873); Leslie Stephen (1881); Edith Simcox (1873); [Unsigned], *Saturday Review*; [R. H. Hutton] (1872), in *Critical Heritage*, 359, 467, 323, 314, 290, 296–7.

Charles Dickens, reported in Philip Collins, *Dickens: Interviews and Recollections* (London, 1983), I, 120.

George Eliot to John Walter Cross, reported in *Interviews and Recollections*, 221–2.

D. A. Miller, *The Novel and the Police* (Berkeley, 1988), 24–5.

[R. H. Hutton] (1872), in *Critical Heritage*, 303.

John Mullan, 'Revisiting the Genius of *Middlemarch*', *Literary Hub* (21 November 2018).

Fredric Jameson, 'George Eliot and *Mauvaise Foi*', in *The Antinomies of Realism* (London, 2013), 114–37.

Simone de Beauvoir, *Memoirs of a Dutiful Daughter*, trans. James Kirkup (New York, 1959), 148.

Swarnakumari Debi Ghosal, *An Unfinished Song [Kahake]* (1898; trans. 1913) (London: 1913), chapter 12.

Ahdaf Soueif, *In the Eye of the Sun* (London, 1992), 298.

Min Jin Lee, *Pachinko* (London, 2017), 306–7.

On Eliot's global reception and colonial educational models, see Oliver Lovesey, *Postcolonial George Eliot* (London, 2017), chapter 5.

On the global status of the 19th-century British realist novel see Elaine Freedgood, *Worlds Enough: The Invention of Realism in the Victorian Novel* (Princeton, 2019), 1, xii, ix.

On Eliot's European reception, see Elinor Shaffer and Catherine Brown (eds), *The Reception of George Eliot in Europe* (London, 2016).

Epilogue

Eliot (1857), *Journals*, 71–2.

Eliot to John Walter Cross, *George Eliot's Life*, I, 36.

[Unsigned], 'George Eliot's Life', *The Times*, 4.

Further reading

The expanding 'George Eliot Archive', <georgeeliotarchive.org>, aims to provide free access to all of Eliot's works, as well as a wide range of responses to her works.

There are two journals devoted to Eliot: the *George Eliot Review* (George Eliot Fellowship, <georgeeliotreview.org>) and *George Eliot–George Henry Lewes Studies* (Penn State University Press).

Useful reference works on Eliot include *George Eliot: A Bibliographical History*, ed. William Baker and John C. Ross (New Castle, DE: Oak Knoll, 2002); Timothy Hands, *A George Eliot Chronology* (London: Macmillan Press, 1989); *Everyone and Everything in George Eliot*, 2 vols, ed. George Newlin (London: Routledge, 2006); and *Oxford Reader's Companion to George Eliot*, ed. John Rignall (Oxford: Oxford University Press, 2000).

Works on Eliot's reception include *George Eliot: The Critical Heritage*, ed. David Carroll (London: Routledge and Kegan Paul, 1971; repr. 2000); *George Eliot: Interviews and Recollections*, ed. K. K. Collins (Basingstoke: Palgrave Macmillan, 2010); Gail Marshall, *Lives of Victorian Literary Figures 1: George Eliot* (London: Pickering and Chatto, 2003); and *The Reception of George Eliot in Europe*, ed. Elinor Shaffer and Catherine Brown (London: Bloomsbury, 2016).

The biography by Gordon S. Haight, *George Eliot: A Biography* (London: Penguin, 1968, repr. 1985) was the first authoritative study and remains enormously valuable. Later biographies include Jenny Uglow, *George Eliot* (London: Virago, 1987); Rosemary

Ashton, *George Eliot: A Life* (London: Hamish Hamilton, 1996); and Kathryn Hughes, *George Eliot: The Last Victorian* (London: Fourth Estate, 1998). Four works that move fluidly between biography and criticism are Avrom Fleishman, *George Eliot's Intellectual Life* (Cambridge: Cambridge University Press, 2010); Rosemarie Bodenheimer, *The Real Life of Mary Ann Evans: George Eliot, Her Letters and Fiction* (Ithaca, NY: Cornell University Press, 1994); Nancy Henry, *The Life of George Eliot: A Critical Biography* (Oxford: Wiley-Blackwell, 2012); and Philip Davis, *The Transferred Life of George Eliot* (Oxford: Oxford University Press, 2017).

The following companions and overviews offer useful critical starting points: Tim Dolin, *Authors in Context: George Eliot* (Oxford: Oxford World's Classics, 2005); *A Companion to George Eliot*, ed. Amanda Anderson and Harry E. Shaw (Oxford: Wiley-Blackwell, 2013; repr. 2016); *The Cambridge Companion to George Eliot*, ed. George Levine and Nancy Henry (Cambridge: Cambridge University Press, 2019); Jill Matus, 'George Eliot', in *The Cambridge Companion to English Novelists*, ed. Adrian Poole (Cambridge: Cambridge University Press, 2009), 225–41; *George Eliot in Context*, ed. Margaret Harris (Cambridge: Cambridge University Press, 2013); and *The Oxford Handbook of George Eliot*, ed. Juliette Atkinson and Elisha Cohn (Oxford: Oxford University Press, 2025).

Collections and overviews of literary criticism include *A Century of George Eliot Criticism*, ed. Gordon S. Haight (London: Methuen, 1966); Fionnuala Dillane, 'George Eliot', in *Oxford Bibliographies Online*; Gail Marshall, 'George Eliot', in *Oxford Bibliographies Online*; *George Eliot: Critical Assessments*, 4 vols, ed. Stuart Hutchinson (Mountfield: Helm, 1996); Lucie Armitt, *George Eliot: Adam Bede, The Mill on the Floss, Middlemarch: A Reader's Guide to Essential Criticism* (Basingstoke: Palgrave, 2000); and *Middlemarch in the Twenty-First Century*, ed. Karen Chase (Oxford: Oxford University Press, 2006).

Influential monographs on Eliot include Gillian Beer, *George Eliot* (Brighton: Harvester Wheatsheaf, 1986); Gillian Beer, *Darwin's Plots: Evolutionary Narrative in Darwin, George Eliot and Nineteenth-Century Fiction* (Cambridge: Cambridge University Press, 1983; repr. 2000); David Carroll, *George Eliot and the Conflict of Interpretations* (Cambridge: Cambridge University Press, 1992); Fionnuala Dillane, *Before George Eliot: Marian*

Evans and the Periodical Press (Cambridge: Cambridge University Press, 2013); Barbara Hardy, *The Novels of George Eliot: A Study in Form* (London: Athlone, 1959); and J. Hillis Miller, *Reading for Our Time: 'Adam Bede' and 'Middlemarch' Revisited* (Edinburgh: Edinburgh University Press, 2012).

Index

Since the index has been created to work across multiple formats, indexed terms for which a page range is given (e.g., 52–53, 66–70, etc.) may occasionally appear only on some, but not all of the pages within the range.

Figures are indicated by an italic *f.*

George Eliot

ENGLISH LITERATURE
A Very Short Introduction
Jonathan Bate

Sweeping across two millennia and every literary genre, acclaimed scholar and biographer Jonathan Bate provides a dazzling introduction to English Literature. The focus is wide, shifting from the birth of the novel and the brilliance of English comedy to the deep Englishness of landscape poetry and the ethnic diversity of Britain's Nobel literature laureates. It goes on to provide a more in-depth analysis, with close readings from an extraordinary scene in King Lear to a war poem by Carol Ann Duffy, and a series of striking examples of how literary texts change as they are transmitted from writer to reader.

{No reviews}

WRITING AND SCRIPT
A Very Short Introduction
Andrew Robinson

Without writing, there would be no records, no history, no books, and no emails. Writing is an integral and essential part of our lives; but when did it start? Why do we all write differently and how did writing develop into what we use today? All of these questions are answered in this *Very Short Introduction*. Starting with the origins of writing five thousand years ago, with cuneiform and Egyptian hieroglyphs, Andrew Robinson explains how these early forms of writing developed into hundreds of scripts including the Roman alphabet and the Chinese characters.

'User-friendly survey.'

Steven Poole, The Guardian

ROMANTICISM
A Very Short Introduction
Michael Ferber

What is Romanticism? In this *Very Short Introduction* Michael Ferber answers this by considering who the romantics were and looks at what they had in common – their ideas, beliefs, commitments, and tastes. He looks at the birth and growth of Romanticism throughout Europe and the Americas, and examines various types of Romantic literature, music, painting, religion, and philosophy. Focusing on topics, Ferber looks at the rising prestige of the poet; Romanticism as a religious trend; Romantic philosophy and science; Romantic responses to the French Revolution; and the condition of women. Using examples and quotations he presents a clear insight into this very diverse movement.

www.oup.com/vsi

BEAUTY
A Very Short Introduction
Roger Scruton

In this *Very Short Introduction* the renowned philosopher Roger Scruton explores the concept of beauty, asking what makes an object - either in art, in nature, or the human form - beautiful, and examining how we can compare differing judgements of beauty when it is evident all around us that our tastes vary so widely. Is there a right judgement to be made about beauty? Is it right to say there is more beauty in a classical temple than a concrete office block, more in a Rembrandt than in last year's Turner Prize winner? Forthright and thought-provoking, and as accessible as it is intellectually rigorous, this introduction to the philosophy of beauty draws conclusions that some may find controversial, but, as Scruton shows, help us to find greater sense of meaning in the beautiful objects that fill our lives.

A fascinating book, which I heartily recommend.

Brya Wilson, Readers Digest

BESTSELLERS
A Very Short Introduction
John Sutherland

'I rejoice', said Doctor Johnson, 'to concur with the Common Reader.' For the last century, the tastes and preferences of the common reader have been reflected in the American and British bestseller lists, and this *Very Short Introduction* takes an engaging look through the lists to reveal what we have been reading - and why. John Sutherland shows that bestseller lists monitor one of the strongest pulses in modern literature and are therefore worthy of serious study. Along the way, he lifts the lid on the bestseller industry, examines what makes a book into a bestseller, and asks what separates bestsellers from canonical fiction.

'His amiable trawl through the history of popular books is frequently entertaining'

Scott Pack, The Times

ENGLISH LANGUAGE
A Very Short Introduction
Simon Horobin

The English language is spoken by more than a billion people throughout the world. But where did English come from? And how has it evolved into the language used today?

In this *Very Short Introduction* Simon Horobin investigates how we have arrived at the English we know today, and celebrates the way new speakers and new uses mean that it continues to adapt. Engaging with contemporary concerns about correctness, Horobin considers whether such changes are improvements, or evidence of slipping standards. What is the future for the English language? Will Standard English continue to hold sway, or we are witnessing its replacement by newly emerging Englishes?

www.oup.com/vsi

RUSSIAN LITERATURE
A Very Short Introduction
Catriona Kelly

Rather than a conventional chronology of Russian literature, Catriona Kelly's *Very Short Introduction* explores the place and importance of diverse literature in Russian culture. How and when did a Russian national literature come into being? What shaped its creation? How have the Russians regarded their literary language? At the centre of the web is the figure of Pushkin, 'the Russian Shakespeare', whose work influenced all Russian writers, whether poets or novelists, and many great artists in other areas as well.

'brilliant and original, taking an unexpected approach to the subject, and written with great confidence and clarity.'

Peter France, University of Edinburgh

'a great pleasure to read. It is a sophisticated, erudite, searching, and subtle piece of work. It is written in a lively and stimulating manner, and displays a range to which few of Dr Kelly's peers in the field of Russian scholarship can aspire.'

Phil Cavendish, School of Slavonic and East European Studies, University of London

www.oup.com/vsi

FRENCH LITERATURE
A Very Short Introduction
John D. Lyons

The heritage of literature in the French language is rich, varied, and extensive in time and space; appealing both to its immediate public, readers of French, and also to aglobal audience reached through translations and film adaptations. *French Literature: A Very Short Introduction* introduces this lively literary world by focusing on texts - epics, novels, plays, poems, and screenplays - that concern protagonists whose adventures and conflicts reveal shifts in literary and social practices. From the hero of the medieval *Song of Roland* to the Caribbean heroines of *Tituba, Black Witch of Salem* or the European expatriate in Japan in *Fear and Trembling*, these problematic protagonists allow us to understand what interests writers and readers across the wide world of French.

GERMAN LITERATURE
A Very Short Introduction
Nicholas Boyle

German writers, from Luther and Goethe to Heine, Brecht,
and Günter Grass, have had a profound influence on the modern
world. This *Very Short Introduction* presents an engrossing tour
of the course of German literature from the late Middle Ages to
the present, focussing especially on the last 250 years.
Emphasizing the economic and religious context of many
masterpieces of German literature, it highlights how they can be
interpreted as responses to social and political changes within
an often violent and tragic history. The result is a new and clear
perspective which illuminates the power of German literature
and the German intellectual tradition, and its impact on the
wider cultural world.

> 'Boyle has a sure touch and an obvious authority ... this is a
> balanced and lively introduction to German literature.'
>
> **Ben Hutchinson, TLS**

WILLIAM SHAKESPEARE
A Very Short Introduction
Stanley ells

In this new offering from Stanley Wells, the pre-eminent Shakespearian scholar, comes an exploration of one of the world's greatest dramatists: William Shakespeare.

Examining Shakespeare's narrative poems, sonnets, and all of his plays, Wells outlines their sources, style, and originality over the course of Shakespeare's career, to consider the fundamental impact his work has had for subsequent generations. Written with enthusiasm and flair by a scholar who has devoted a lifetime to the study of Shakespeare and his works, this is an engaging and authoritative introduction that looks at both the world Shakespeare lived in and all of his major works, to show how and why he continues to be so influential and important to society today.

"this is an excellent place to start exploring the life and work of probably the most celebrated dramatist not only in Britain but also throughout the world." - Shiny New Books

www.oup.com/vsi

SHAKESPEARE'S SONNETS AND POEMS

A Very Short Introduction

Jonathan F. S. Post

William Shakespeare is considered possibly the most famous writer in history; his works have had a lasting effect on culture, vocabularies, and art. His plays contain some of our most well-known lines (how often have you heard the phrase 'To be or not to be'?), yet whilst his poems may often feel less familiar than his plays, they have also seeped into our cultural history (who has not heard of 'Shall I compare thee to a summer's day'?).

In this *Very Short Introduction*, Jonathan Post introduces all of Shakespeare's poetry: the Sonnets; the two great narrative poems, *Venus and Adonis* and *The Rape of Lucrece*; *A Lover's Complaint*; and *The Phoenix and Turtle*. Describing Shakespeare's double identity as both poet and playwright, in conjunction with several of his contemporaries, Post evaluates the reciprocal advantages as well as the different strategies and strains that came with writing for the stage and the page. Tackling the debates surrounding the disputed authorship of Shakespeare's poems, he also considers the printing history of Shakespeare's canon, and the genres favoured by the bard. Exploring their reception, both with contemporary audiences and through the ages until today, Post explores the core themes of love and lust, and analyzes how the sonnets compare with other great love poetry of the English Renaissance.

www.oup.com/vsi

KNOWLEDGE
A Very Short Introduction
Jennifer Nagel

What is knowledge? Is it the same as opinion or truth? Do you need to be able to justify a claim in order to count as knowing it?

Questions like these are ancient ones, and the branch of philosophy dedicated to answering them—epistemology—has been active for thousands of years.

In this thought provoking *Very Short Introduction*, Jennifer Nagel considers the central problems and paradoxes in the theory of knowledge whilst drawing attention to the ways in which philosophers and theorists have responded to them. She incorporates methods from logic, linguistics, and psychology, and uses a number of everyday examples to demonstrate the key issues and debates.